Daniel McDonald

Removal of the Pottawattomie Indians from northern Indiana; embracing also a brief statement of the Indian policy of the government, and other historical matter relating to the Indian question

Vol. 1

Daniel McDonald

Removal of the Pottawattomie Indians from northern Indiana; embracing also a brief statement of the Indian policy of the government, and other historical matter relating to the Indian question
Vol. 1

ISBN/EAN: 9783337304973

Printed in Europe, USA, Canada, Australia, Japan

Cover: Foto ©ninafisch / pixelio.de

More available books at **www.hansebooks.com**

REMOVAL

OF THE

POTTAWATTOMIE INDIANS

FROM

NORTHERN INDIANA

EMBRACING ALSO A BRIEF STATEMENT OF THE INDIAN
POLICY OF THE GOVERNMENT, AND OTHER
HISTORICAL MATTER RELATING TO
THE INDIAN QUESTION.

BY—

DANIEL McDONALD.

———

"A mixed occupancy of the same territory by the white and red man is incompatible
with the safety or happiness of either * * * The remedial policy, the principles of which
were settled more than thirty years ago under the administration of Mr. Jefferson, consists of an extinction, for a fair consideration, of the titles to all the lands still occupied
by the Indians within the states and territories of the United States, their removal to a
country west of the Mississippi much more extensive and better adapted to their condition than they now occupy * * * "—FROM PRESIDENT VAN BUREN'S MESSAGE.

—

PLYMOUTH, INDIANA:
D. McDONALD & CO., PRINTERS AND BINDERS.
1899

INDEX.

INDEX—Continued.

INDEX—Continued.

ILLUSTRATIONS.

INTRODUCTION.

The question of the extinguishment of the Indian titles to the lands of the Pottawattomie Indians in Northern Indiana and Southern Michigan and their removal to a reservation to be provided for them west of the Missouri river, was one of the most important and delicate questions the government had to deal with in the early settlement of this part of the Northwest territory. General treaties were made from 1820 to 1830 between the government agents and the chiefs and headmen of the Pottawattomies in this part of the country by which large tracts of land were ceded to the government, and numerous reservations made to various bands of Pottawattomies in Northern Indiana and Southern Michigan. Later these reservations were ceded by treaty by the Indians to the government for a stipulated amount, and in all the treaties it was provided that the Indians should remove to the reservation west of the Missouri within two years from the date thereof. The dates of these treaties were about all in the years 1835 and 1836, the last date for removal expiring about the first of August, 1838.

In the numerous treaties and historical sketches which have been written concerning the early settlement of this part of the country up to the present time, but little information has been given in regard to this interesting question. The story which follows was a paper prepared by the writer for, and delivered to, the Northern Indiana Historical Society of South Bend, in the early part of 1898. It was so well received by the society and the large and intelligent audience who heard it, that it has been deemed of sufficient historical interest to preserve it in this form.

THE STORY OF THE REMOVAL.

The territory now included within the boundaries of Indiana, Illinois and Michigan, which was the home of the Pottawattomie Indians for many years prior to the time they were removed to a reservation west of the Missouri river—the cause for which removal will appear hereafter—was in the early days of the history of America owned and occupied by the Miami Indians, originally known as the Twightwees. It was claimed by France from the time of the discovery of the mouth of the Mississippi river by La Salle in 1682 to 1763 when it was relinquished by treaty to the government of England and held by it until 1779 as a part of her colonial possessions in North America. The state of Virginia extended its jurisdiction over it until 1783 when it came by treaty of peace and by deed of cession from Virginia the property of the United States. In 1787 an ordinance was passed by congress creating the territory Northwest of the River Ohio, which embraced the territory of the now states above mentioned.

The Miami Indians.

The Miami Indians, the original inhabitants of this region, were a powerful nation, and about 1790 could muster about 1500 warriors. They were at war with the whites more or less until they were disastrously defeated by Gen. Anthony Wayne in 1794, after which they made peace at Greenville in 1795. After that they rapidly declined. By a series of treaties between that date and 1809 they ceded lands extending from the Wabash river to the Ohio state line. The annuities proved fatal to them, introducing intoxicating liquors, resulting in dissipation, indolence and violence. In the war of 1812 they sided with England and being defeated under Gen. Harrison, they sued for peace, and a treaty was made September 15, 1815. War had broken up the progress they had previously made; drunkenness and debauchery again prevailed, leading to fights in which nearly 500 perished in fifteen years. In 1822, as shown by the census, they numbered 2,000 or 3,000 on three reservations. The Wea or Pin-kee-shaw bands numbering 384 were removed—or rather removed themselves, in 1833-5 to a reservation of 160,000 acres of land in Kansas. The Miamis, then numbering about 1.100 all told, sold to the government 177,000 acres in Indiana for $335,680, still retaining a considerable tract, but by treaties made in 1838 and 1840 they ceded to the grovernment practically all these reservations and were removed to near Fort Levenworth, Kansas. At that time they had dwindled to a wretched, dissipated band of 250, each individual being paid an annuity of about \$125. In 1873 they numbered about 150, and now that once great and powerful nation originally in possession of the whole of the territory of what is now Indiana, Illinois and Southern Michigan, is practically extinct.

The Pottawattomie Indians.

In the early days the Miamis permitted the Pottawattomies to occupy their lands in Northern Indiana, Illinois and Southern Michigan, and finally they were recognized by the owners of the territory occupied by them, and with them, after the United States came in possession of the territory through the ordinance of 1787, treaties were made by which all the lands were finally ceded to the United States.

The Pottawattomie tribe of Indians, the owners and inhabitants of the territory now composing Northern Indiana, belonged to the great Al-gon-quin family, and were related by ties of consanguinity to the Ojibways or Chipewas and Ottowas. The first trace we have of them locates their territory in the Lake Superior region on the islands near the entrance to Green Bay, holding the country from the latter point to the head waters of the great lakes. Subsequently they adopted into their tribe many of the Ottowas from Upper Canada.

In the name of this tribe there is a marked significance touching certain characteristics from which they acquire some early distinction. The name is said by a writer on Indian lore to be a compound of Putta-wa, signifying a blowing out or expansion of the checks as in blowing a fire; and "Me" a nation, which, being interpreted means a nation of fire-blowers. The application seems to have orignated in the facility with which they produced flame and set burning the ancient council fires of their forefathers beside the waters of the Green Bay country.

About 1817 it was estimated that there were in the region north of the Wabash river and south of Lake Michigan something more than 2,000 Pottawattomies. They were located at villages on the Tippecanoe, Kankakee, Iroquois, Yellow river, St. Joseph of Lake Michigan, the Elkhart, Miamis of the Lake, the St. Joseph emptying into it, the St. Marys, Twin Lakes, Muk-sen-cuck-ee and Lake Kewana. At that time they had no uniform abiding place of residence. During the fall, winter, and part of the spring they were scattered in the woods hunting and fishing. Their wigwams were made of poles stuck in the ground and tied together with slips of bark, slender hickory wythes or rawhide strings. They were covered with bark or a kind of a mat made of flags. There was an occasional rude hut made of logs or poles, but nearly all the dwellings were wigwams hastily put up as here described.

They raised some corn, but lived principally on wild game, fish, fruits, nuts, roots, and were clothed with blankets and untanned skins.

The Treaty of Greenville--1795.

After Gen. Anthony Wayne had subdued the Indians in 1794, he succeeded in concluding a treaty with the various tribes at Greenville, Ohio, in 1795. The boundary lines which were established by that treaty between the United States and the bands of the Northwestern tribes, gave to the Indians all the territory lying within the present limits of Indiana, with the following exceptions: Six miles square where Ft. Wayne now stands; two miles square on the Wabash river at the end of the portage from the head of the river Maumee eight miles west of Ft. Wayne; six miles square at Ouetenon, or old Wea town; 150,000 acres near the falls of the Ohio, the same being known as "Clark's grant;" the town of Vincennes and adjacent lands to which Indian titles had been extinguished, and all similar lands at other places in possession of the French people, or other white settlers among them and a strip of land running directly from the site of Fort Recovery so as to intersect the river Ohio at a point opposite the mouth of the Kentucky river.

Indian Policy of the Government.

The most important question this country had to deal with in the days of the formation of the republic in regard to Indian affairs was, as to what policy should be adopted and pursued in regard to the future disposition of the various Indian tribes and bands.

In his second inaugural address in 1821, President Monroe brought the question of the care and disposition of the Indian tribes before congress. Up to that time the government had treated them as separate and independent nations. "The distinction," said President Monroe, "had flattered their pride, retarded their improvement, and in many instances paved the way for their destruction." Continuing he said: "They have claims on the magnanimity—on the justice of this nation which we must all feel, and we should become their real benefactors. Their sovereignty over vast territories should cease, in lieu of which the right of soil should be granted, to be invested in permanent funds for the support of civil government over them and for the education of their children, for their instruction in the arts of husbandry, and to provide sustenance for them until they can provide it for themselves."

In conformity to this recommendation congress soon after made appropriations and appointed commissioners to negotiate treaties with the various tribes. In 1824 president Monroe in his inaugural message again stated that the object had not been effected, but added: "Many of the tribes have already made great progress in the arts of civilization and civilized life. This desirable result has been brought about by the humane and persevering policy of the government, and particularly by the proposition for the civilization of the Indians. There have been established under the provisions of this act 32 schools, containing 916 scholars who are well instructed in several branches of literature, and likewise in agriculture and the ordinary arts of life. Their civilization is indispensible to their safety, and this can be accomplished only by degrees. Difficulties of the most serious character present themselves to the attainment of this very desirable result on the territory on which they now reside. To remove them by force even with a view to their own security and happiness would be revolting to humanity and unjustifiable." He therefore recommended that the territory embraced within the limits of the states and territories and the Rocky mountains, and Mexico should be divided into districts to which the Indians should be induced to emigrate.

In a special message to congress in 1825 President Monroe again said: "The great object to be accomplished is the removal of these tribes to the territory designated on conditions which shall be satisfactory to themselves and honorable to the United States. This can be done only by conveying to each tribe a good title to an adequate portion of land to which it may consent to remove, and by providing for it there a system of internal government which shall protect their property from invasion and by the regular progress of improvement and civilization prevent that degeneracy which has generally marked the transition from the one to the other state."

In his second annual message dated December 6th, 1830, President Andrew Jackson, on this subject said:

"It gives me pleasure to announce to congress that the benevolent policy of the government steadily pursued for nearly thirty years in relation to the removal of the Indians beyond the white settlement is approaching to a happy consummation. Two important tribes have accepted the provisions made for their removal at the last session of congress, and it is believed their example will induce the remaining tribes also to seek the same obvious advantages." "Doubtless," he continued "it will be painful to leave the graves of their fathers; but what do they more than our ancestors did or their children are now doing? To better their condition in an unknown land our forefathers left all that was dear in earthly objects. Our children by thousands yearly leave the land of their birth to seek new homes in distant regions. Does humanity weep at these painful separations from everything animate and inanimate with which the young heart has become entwined? It is rather a source of joy that our country affords scope where our young population may range unconstrained in body or mind, developing the power and faculties of the man in their highest perfection. These remove hundreds and almost thousands of miles at their own expense, purchase the lands they occupy and support themselves at their new homes from the moment of their arrival. Can it be cruel in this government, when by events which it cannot control, the Indian is made discontented in his ancient home to purchase his lands, to give him a new and extensive territory, to pay the expense of his removal and support him a year in his new abode? How many thousands of our people would gladly embrace the opportunity of removing west on such conditions?"

In his message in 1831 he said:

"My opinion remains the same, and I can see no other alternative for the Indians but that of their removal to the west or a quiet submission to the state laws."

That policy the government adhered to to the end, and in accordance therewith all subsequent treaties were made.

The Treaty of 1826.

On October 16, 1826, Lewis Cass, James B. Ray and John Tipton concluded a treaty with the Pottawattomie tribe by which a large scope of country in Southern Michigan and Northern Indiana, was ceded to the United States, from which numerous small reservations were made, in all containing ninety-nine sections. The Indians were to receive an annuity of $2,000 in silver for the term of twenty-two years, and the government was to support a blacksmith shop at some convenient point, and to appropriate for educational purposes annually $2,000 as long as congress might think proper; also to build for them a mill, sufficient for them to grind corn, on the Tippecanoe river, and provide for the support of a miller. This mill was built on the outlet of Mana-tou lake a short distance east of the present town of Rochester. The government was also to pay them annually 160 bushels of salt, all to be paid by the Indian agent at Fort Wayne.

The Michigan Road Treaty.

Into this treaty was interjected an article in which was ceded to the State of Indiana a strip of land one hundred feet wide extending from Lake Michigan at Michigan City to Madison on the Ohio river. The article is as follows:

"ARTICLE 2. As an evidence of the attachment which the Pottawattomie tribe feel towards the American people, and particularly to the soil of Indiana, and with a view to demonstrate their liberality, and benefit themselves by creating facilities for traveling and increasing the value of their remaining country, the said tribe do hereby cede to the United States a strip of land commencing at Lake Michigan and running thence to the Wabash river, one hundred feet wide, for a road, and also, one section of good land contiguous to the said road for each mile of the same, and also for each mile of a road from the termination thereof through Indianapolis to the Ohio river for the purpose of making a road aforesaid from Lake Michigan by the way of Indianapolis to some convenient point on the Ohio river. And the general assembly of the State of Indiana shall have a right to locate the said road and to apply said sections, or the proceeds thereof to the making of the same, and the said grant shall be at their sole disposal."

The wording of the treaty was a cunningly devised arrangement to swindle the Indians of an immense amount of some of the best lands belonging to them in the state. The Indians had nothing to do with writing the treaty, and evidently knew little about what the result of its operation would be. They were lead to believe that a great thoroughfare between Lake Michigan and the Ohio river would be built which would enable them to travel with ease and comfort between these two important points.

Congress having confirmed the treaty the legislature in 1830 ordered the line to be surveyed and laid out. By reference to the state map, it will be observed that the road did not run in a direct line across the state. From Indianapolis north it leads directly to Logansport, thence through Rochester and Plymouth to South Bend. At the latter place it turns directly west and runs through the St. Joseph and Laporte prairies and thence to the mouth of Trail creek at Michigan City.

By the act of the legislature approved in 1832 a commissioner to manage the construction of the road and dispose of the lands was created. In regard to the construction of the road north of Logansport it was provided as follows:

"SEC. 11. Said commissioner is hereby authorized and required to have that part of the Michigan road that lies between the town of Logansport and Lake Michigan at the mouth of Trail Creek, cut and opened one hundred feet wide. between the 15th day of June next and the last day of November next, in the manner following to-wit: Cut and clear off of the said road, all logs, timber and undergrowth, leaving no stump more than one foot above the level of the earth: the creek banks to be graded, and the swamps and mud causewayed, and good, sufficient bridge made over such streams and swamps as is necessary to make the same passable at all times for wagons, and as near as may be every part equally good. *Provided*, however, that the expenditure on said road, north of Logansport, shall not exceed in the aggregate, the amount that has been expended and is by this act appropriated on said road south of Logansport to the Ohio river, in proportion to the distance.

"SEC. 12. Said commissoner shall cause that part of said road between Logansport and Lake Michigan to be laid off in sections of one

FIRST FRAME HOUSE ERECTED NORTH OF WABASH RIVER.

Residence of William Polke, near Tippecanoe River, on Michigan Road, North of Rochester; Built in 1832.

mile each, to be numbered in numerical order, one, two, three, and so on, commencing at Logansport; and said commissioner is hereby authorized to make such alterations in said road as he shall deem necessary within the land selected and surveyed for said road, and through such lands as the road may pass; such other alterations may be made as may be deemed beneficial and lessen the expenses of opening the same, and not materially increase the distance with the consent of the owners of such lands; and the commissioner is authorized to receive relinquishments to the state for the use of the road the width one hundred feet for said road, and said commissioner is authorized to make such alteration at Michigan City, a town lately laid off at the termination of said road on Lake Michigan, so as to enter Michigan street and pass along the same and Wabash street in said town to the termination of said road."

The road was completed after a fashion through Northern Indiana in the latter part of 1833 and the early part of 1834. Judge William Polke, who was appointed by the government removing agent and took charge of the last removal in 1838, at Danville, Illinois, was a large contractor in building the road. At that time he resided in the first frame house erected north of the Wabash river which stood, and yet stands in an excellent state of preservation on the east side of the Michigan road about a mile north of the Tippecanoe river. It was near this house and not far from the Tippecanoe river at the Indian village called Chip-pe-way, where Gen. Tipton and his soldiers camped with 859 Indians the first night after leaving Twin lakes in Marshall county when they were being removed to the reservation provided for them by the government west of the Missouri river. This was Sept. 2d, 1838.

The Polke Family.

William Polke was a very prominent man in the affairs of the early settlement of this state, and especially of Northern Indiana. He accumulated large landed interests and was one of the original proprietors of Plymouth, and probably other towns along the line of the Michigan road. About the time of the admission of the state into the Union he took an active interest in the civilization of the Indians, and for a time assisted Rev. Isaac McCoy, Baptist missionary then stationed at the Carey mission near where Niles, Michigan, is now located, in pacifying and subduing the war-like spirit of the Indians of this part of the state and Southern Michigan. He did much to bring about the extinguishment of the Indian titles but never served as agent for the government in perfecting any of the treaties in this part of the state.

In 1878, John C. McCoy, of Wilder, Johnson county, Kansas, a son of Rev. Isaac McCoy, wrote a letter to Rev. G. H. Bailey, of Niles, in which he details some incidents of striking historical interest, in connection with the Polke family. He says:

"My mother's maiden name was Christiana Polke, one of the younger children of Charles Polke. In 'Jefferson's Notes,' a small book by President Jefferson, is a certificate from the same Charles Polke to prove the charge against Col. Cresap for the murder of the family of the celebrated Indian chief Logan. He then lived in southwestern Pennsylvania. He afterward moved to Nelson county, Ky., where my mother was born. Before the birth of my mother the Indians captured the stockade fort, 'Kinchelor's Station,' in which the settlers were collected (most of the men being absent at the time), killed the few men and many of the women and children, destroying everything, and carried away the surviving women and children as prisoners. Among these were the wife and three children of my grandfather, Charles Polke. These children were Judge William Polke, afterwards a prominent man in Indiana, Nancy, Ruby, and Eleanor Hollingsworth. They were taken to Detroit, where the British held

MRS. CHRISTIANA McCOY.
[From a photograph obtained by Capt. Orville F. Chamberlin, of Elkhart, from Mrs. Harris, a granddaughter of Mrs. McCoy.]

possession, and where she (Mrs. Polk) was delivered of another child (Thomas), who died about one year ago (1877) a wealthy citizen of Texas.

"My grandmother was ransomed from the Indians by some benevolent British officer, and remained for about three years in Detroit, supporting herself and child by her needle   The three other children were carried off by the Pottawattomie Indians to the St. Joseph river, probably in the vicinity of the Carey Mission (Niles).

"For three long years my grandfather supposed they had all been slain in the massacre at the burning fort. At last my grandmother found means to send him word of their condition. He traveled alone on foot through the trackless wilderness three hundred miles in search of his lost ones whom God had spared. He was treated with great kindness by the British officials, who gave him such aid for the recovery of his children as he desired. He went alone, and at last found them, two with one family of the Pottawattomies and one with another, by whom they were adopted. When grandfather found the two first, William and Eleanor, and they knew he had come for them, they both ran and hid themselves. They had forgotten their native tongue, and it was with difficulty that he finally induced their foster-parents to give them up or them to accompany him. This transpired certainly but a few miles from the site of the old Carey Mission, where years afterwards another child, and sister of these lost captives, went through toil and tempest to repay the very same people (many of whom were still living), not with vengeance or injury, but with gifts of richer and more enduring value than gold."

Treaties Between 1795 and 1832.

From the date of the treaty of peace at Greenville in 1795 to 1832 all the lands in possession of the Pottawattomie and Miami Indians were ceded to the United States by treaties made between the chiefs on behalf of the Indians, and commissioners appointed by the government on behalf of the United States. Nearly all the titles to the lands in this part of the country reserved for various bands by the treaty of 1832 were extinguished by United States Commissioner Abel C. Pepper who seems to have had a powerful influence over the wild men of the forest. He was born in Shenandoah county, Virginia, settled in Rising Sun, Indiana, prior to the admission into the Union in 1816, and in various ways took an active interest in the formation of the new state and preventing them from committing depredations. He died in Rising Sun March 20, 1860.

In the year 1831 the legislature of Indiana passed a joint resolution requesting an appropriation by congress for the purpose of the extinguishment of the remaining Indian titles of lands within the state. The appropriation was made and three citizens—Jonathan Jennings, first Governor of Indiana, John W. Davis and Marks Crume were appointed by the secretary of war to carry into effect the law authorizing the appropriation. These commissioners assembled with the several Indian chiefs concerned at a place called Chippeway, or Chippeway-nung on the Tippecanoe river where the Michigan road crosses the same, two or three miles north of Rochester, and sixteen miles south of Plymouth, where they concluded a treaty October 27, 1832, by which the chiefs and warriors of the Pottawattomies of Indiana and Michigan territory ceded to the United States their title and interest to all the lands in Indiana, Michigan and Illinois south of Grand River. From this general treaty a large number of small individual reservations were made. Among them was a reservation of two sections to Nas-wau-gee, and one section to Quash-qua, both on the east shore of Lake Muk-sen-cuck-ee; 22 sections to Menominee, Pe-pin-a-wa, Na-ta-ka and Mac-a-taw-ma-aw, taking in Twin Lakes;—several sections on the east and south of Lake Muk-sen-cuck-ee to Au-be-nau-be, in all, in this and Fulton county, 36 sections, and to other chiefs making total reservations of 160 sections. These reservations were all ceded back to the government between 1834-7 by treaties, mostly negotiated by Abel C. Pepper. William Marshall concluded a treaty with Chief Com-o-za Dec. 4, 1834, on the lake which is spelled Max-ee-nie-kue-kee. April 11th Col. Pepper negotiated a treaty with Pau-koo-shuck on the Tippecanoe river for the 36 sections owned by Au-be-nau-be, his father, whom he had killed in his cabin near the Tippecanoe river.

Table of Treaties.

The following is a table of all the treaties by which the individual reservations in Marshall and adjoining counties were ceded to the government, being the reservations made to the several chiefs named by the treaty of 1832:

Date.	Place.	Commissioner.	Chief.	No. Secs.
Dec. 4, 1834	Maxeeniekuekee....	Wm. Marshall...	Com-o-za.........	2
Dec. 10, '34	Tippecanoe........	" "	Muck-kose........	6
Dec. 17, '34	Logansport........	" "	Mo-ta	4
Mar. 26, '36	Turkey Creek......	Abel C. Pepper..	Mus-qua-buck.....	4
Mar. 29, '36	Tippecanoe River...	" "	Wa-ke-wa.........	4
Apr. 11, '36	" "	" "	Pau-koo-shuck.....	36
Apr. 22, '36	Logansport Agency	" "	Au-ka-maus, Ke-way-nee, Ne-bosh, Mat-chis-jaw.....	10
Apr. 22, '36	" "	" "	Quash-qua, Nas-wau-gee	3
Sep. 20, '36	Chipewaynung......	" "	Me-met-wa, Che-qua-ke-ko	10
Aug. 5, '36	Yellow River.	" "	Pe-pin-a-wa, Na-ta-ka, Mack-a-taw-ma-ah	22
Sept. 23, '36	Chipewaynung......	" "	Krin-krash........	4
Sept. 23, '36	" "	" "	Che-chaw-kose	10
Sept. 23, '36	" "	" "	As-kum, We-si-on-as	10
Sept. 23, '36	" "	" "	We-saw	4
Sept. 23, '36	" "	" "	Mo-ta, Min-o-quet, Mosac	12
Feb. 11, '37	Washington	J. T. Douglass...	Che-chaw-kose, As-kum, We-saw, Muck-rose, Que-ko-to, all the interest of which they were possessed.	

The last treaty the government concluded with the Pottawattomies was made at Washington City by John T. Douglass on the part of the United States and Chee-chaw-kose, Ask-um, We-saw, or Louison, Muk-kose, and Qui-qui-to chiefs. This treaty was a ratification of all the treaties concluded by Abel C. Pepper, August 5th and September 23d, 1836, in which were ceded the lands reserved for them in the treaty of October 26-7, 1832. The said chiefs agreed that they and their several bands would remove to the country that would be provided for them by the government southwest of the Missouri river within two years from the date of the treaty. It was also further provided as follows:

."ARTICLE 3.—The United States further agrees to convey by patent to the Pottawattomies of Indiana a tract of country on the Osage river, southwest of the Missouri river, sufficient in extent and adapted to their wants and habits, remove them to the same; furnish them with one year's subsistence after their arrival there, and pay the expenses of the treaty, and of the delegation now in this city."

All the treaties previously made by which the Indians surrendered their titles to the lands reserved for them by the treaty of 1832 also contained a provision that they would remove to the reservation west of the Missouri within two years.

First Emigration From Northern Indiana.

The first emigration of the Pottawattomies from Northern Indiana under the treaty stipulations made in 1836 that they would remove to their reservation within two years took place in July, 1837. Under the direction of Abel C. Pepper U. S. Commissioner, the small bands of Ke-wa-na, Ne-bosh, Nas-wau-gee, and a few others assembled at the village now known as Ke-wa-na, in Fulton county. They were placed in charge of a man by the name of George Proffit who conducted them to their reservation. In this emigration there were about one hundred all told, all of whom went voluntarily. Among the chiefs who were well known was Nas-wau-gee. He ruled over a little band at his village on the east shore of Lake Muk-sen-cuck-ee not far from the residence of the late Henry H. Culver, founder of Culver military academy. He owned a reserve of two sections which he ceded to the government in 1836, and agreed to remove with his band to the country west of the Missouri within two years from the date of the treaty.

Nas-wau-gee was a quiet, peaceable chief, and made friends with all the white settlers in the region about. When the time came to leave he determined to go peaceably, as he had agreed he would. The day before he started he sent word to all the white settlers to come to his village, as he wished to bid them farewell. A large number assembled, and through an interpreter he said substantially:

"*My White Brethren*:— I have called you here to bid you farewell. Myself and my band start at sunrise tomorrow morning to remove to an unknown country the government of the United States has provided for us west of the Missouri river. I have sold my lands to the government and we agreed to leave within two years. That time is about to expire, and according to the agreement we have made we must leave you and the scenes near and dear to all of us. The government has treated us fairly and it is our duty to live up to that contract by doing as we agreed, and so we must go. The white settlers here have been good and kind to us, and in leaving them it seems like severing the ties of our own kindred and friends. We go away and may never return, but wherever we may be—wherever our lot in life may be cast, we shall always remember you with sincere feellings of respect and esteem."

The old chief was visibly affected and tears were seen to flow from his eyes. All the people present took him by the hand and bade him a final adieu as well as most of the members of his band. Early the next morning with their personal effects packed on their ponies, they marched away in single file following the Indian trail along the east shore to the south end of Muksencuckee thence southwest to Ke wa-na, where they joined the other bands and immediately proceeded on their long and wearisome journey.

On the 6th of August, 1838, the time stipulated in the several treaties for the Indians to emigrate having expired, and many declining to go, a council was held at the Me-no-mi-nee village just north of Twin Lakes in Marshall county, five miles southwest from Plymouth, in July or August, 1838. Col. Abel C. Pepper, agent of the government was present and most of the chiefs in that part of the county, also many white residents of the surrounding country. The treaties were read wherein it was shown that in ceding their lands the Indians had agreed to remove to the western reservation within the time specified, and that the date was then at hand when they must go. It was plain to those present who were familiar with the Indian character that there was great dissatisfaction among them and a spirit of rebellion growing which if not soon suppressed would probably lead to serious results. The leader and principal spokesman for the Indians was Me-no-mi-nee. By the treaty of 1832, twenty-two sections of land had been reserved to him and three other chiefs, viz: Pe-pin-a-waw, Na-ta-ka, and Mack-a-taw-ma-ah. This reservation bordered on the west of Plymouth and far enough south to take in Twin Lakes about half way between Plymouth and Muk-sen-cuck-ee Lake. The last three named chiefs entered into a treaty with Col. Abel C. Pepper on behalf of the government August 5th, 1836, by which they ceded all their interest in the reservation above described, for which the government agreed to pay them $14,080 in specie, and they were to remove to the country west of the Missouri river provided for them within two years. Chief Me-no-mi-nee refused to sign the treaty, and persistently declined to release to the government his interest in the reservation. When Col. Pepper had made his final appeal and all had had their say, Me-no-mi-nee rose to his feet, and drawing his costly blanket around him is reported by one who was present to have said in substance as follows:

"Ki micheozima dodagemagad kageto kidenima kigaget. Win dowa nin waiegima ondji. Windodagemagad kidenima tchi kin sindabin-igansiwanimo achi tchinin kawika migwan lagina tchi. Windadasem-

agad kidenima tchi kin ojtchigade nind oshki ogimag giwshka he achi
awiidis tchi abindis uin. Nind dodagemagad kidenima tchi nin diawa
miwima tchi atawa ninawke achi beka miwia. Win songendomowin
kageto gaskiewisiwin nin ikonjowa kewin kibchibegamog kinidaniss
ogema awenan apinchi mawchi manito ka nind pagidina tchi bi badjim
nind kin minisino inendamowin nin sasiddina takobinige dowa animoosh
kishpin kekendge widebewin. Nin awena wi michi ogima win gwaiak-
obimadis dash win pissinam tchi ikkitiwin ni noshke ogi mog ke
aidwapinwabo; achi anpe win kikegige debwewin win lenddam nagana
nen tchin nin dokee. Ninian kageto aniawe nin aukee. Nin inemdam
kadeto Awtawe inew. Nin aian kagen ijinikasowin debwewin man-
sinaigan, achi memdam kageto injinkaswain pazhig ninaw kegeto miwi
tchi nagana nidokee achi nin kageto manes tchi nomdam mina wa."

Which being interpreted is as follows:

"Members of the Council:—The president does not know the truth.
He like me has been imposed upon. He does not know that your
treaty is a lie, and that I never signed it. He does not know that you
made my young chiefs drunk and got their consent, and pretended to
get mine. He does not know that I have refused to sell my lands and
still refuse. He would not by force drive me from my home the
graves of my tribe, and my children who have gone to the Great Spirit,
nor allow you to tell me your braves will take me, tied like a dog if he
knew the truth. My brother, the President, is just, but he listens to
the word of the young chiefs who have lied; and when he knows the
truth he will leave me to my own. I have not sold my lands. I will
not sell them. I have not signed any treaty and will not sign any.
I am not going to leave my lands and I don't want to hear anything
more about it."

Describing the scene, one who was present said: "Amid the ap-
plause of the chiefs he sat down. Spoken in the peculiar style of the
Indian orator—although repeated by an interpreter—with an eloquence
of which Logan would have been proud, his presence the personifica-
tion of dignity, it presented one of those rare occasions of which history gives but few instances, and on the man of true appreciation would
have made a most profound impression."

Considerable time was spent in trying to persuade Me-no-mi-nee
and his following to accept the inevitable and remove peaceably to the
reservation provided for them, as if they did not, the government would
be compelled to remove them by force. Without accomplishing anything, however, the council disbanded. Me-no-mi-nee was a wise and
experienced chief, and he knew that the final consummation was near
at hand. As soon as the council had disbanded he began at once to
fire the hearts of his followers with a determination to resist the government officers in their evident intention to remove them, peaceably if

they could, forcibly if they must. The consequence was, the Indians became desperate, intoxicating liquors were drank to excess; threats of violence were freely made, and the white settlers in the immediate neighborhood became greatly alarmed for the safety of themselves and families. In this alarming condition of affairs, a number of white settlers of Marshall county early in August 1838 petitioned the governor of Indiana for protection against what they believed would result in the certain destruction of their lives and property. In his message to the legislature December 4, 1838, Governor Wallace said:

"By the conditions of the late treaty with the Pottawattomie tribe of Indians in Indiana, the time stipulated for their departure to the west of the Mississippi expired on the 6th of August last. As this trying moment approached a strong disposition was manifested by many of the most influential among them to disregard the treaty entirely, and to cling to the homes and graves of their fathers at all hazards. In consequence of such a determination on their part, a collision of the most serious character was likely to ensue between them and the surrounding settlers. Apprehensive of such a result, and with a view to prevent it, the citizens of Marshall county, early in the month of August, forwarded to the executive a petition praying that an armed force might be immediately sent to their protection. On receipt of this petition I repaired as speedily as circumstances would permit to the scene of difficulty, in order to satisfy myself by a personal examination whether their fears were justifiable or not. On my return to Logansport a formal requisition awaited me from the Indian Agent, Col. A. C. Pepper, for one hundred armed volunteers to be placed under the command of some competent citizen of the state whose duty it should be to preserve the peace, and to arrest the growing spirit of hostility displayed by the Indians. The requisition was instantly granted. I appointed the Hon. John Tipton to this command, and gave him authority to raise the necessary number of volunteers. He promptly and patriotically accepted the appointment, and although sickness and disease prevailed to an alarming extent throughout northern Indiana, yet such was the spirit and patriotism of the people there, that in about forty-eight hours after the requisition was authorized, the requisite force was not only mustered, but was transported into the midst of the Indians before they were aware of its approach, or before even they could possibly take steps to resist or repel it. The rapidity of the movement, the known decision and energy of Gen. Tipton, backed by his intimate acquaintance and popularity with the Indians, whom it was his business to quiet, accomplished everything desired. The refractory became complacent; opposition to removal ceased; and the whole tribe, with a few exceptions, amounting to between 800 and 900 voluntarily prepared to emigrate. Gen. Tipton and the volunteers ac-

companied them as far as Danville, Illinois, administering to them on
the way whatever comfort and relief humanity required. There they
were delivered over to the care of Judge Polke and the United States removing agents. Copies of all the communications and reports made to
the executive by Gen. Tipton while in the discharge of this duty I lay
before you, from which I feel assured you will discover with myself
that much credit and many thanks are due not only to him but to all
who assisted him in bringing so delicate an affair to so happy and successful a termination."

(Diligent search and inquiry has been made in the several depart-
ments of the state at Indianapolis, and it is much to be regretted that
none of the papers referred to have been preserved.)

Governor David Wallace.

David Wallace was Governor of Indiana from 1837 to 1840. He
was the father of General Lew Wallace, author of "Ben Hur." He
was born in Pennsylvania April 24, 1799, and graduated from West
Point in 1821. He served in the legislature in 1828, 1829 and 1831.
and as Lieutenant-Governor from 1831 to 1836 and Governor 1837 to
1840. During his term as Governor he issued the first Thanksgiving
Day proclamation. The most important act of his administration was
his order to remove the remaining Pottawattomie Indians, as set forth
in his message above quoted. Governor Wallace, after his term as
Governor expired, was subsequently elected to Congress. He was made
a member of the Committee of Ways and Means and in that committee gave the casting vote in favor of assisting with a donation to Pro-
fessor Morse to develop the magnetic telegraph. This vote was rid-
iculed by his political opponents and cost him many votes the last time
he ran for Congress. But he lived to see the telegraph established in
nearly all the countries of the world, and the wisdom of his action acknowledged by all.

As an orator Governor Wallace had few equals. One who knew
him well speaking of his oratorical powers said: "With a voice modu-
lated to the finest and nicest precision, an eye sparkling and expressive,
a countenance and person remarkable for beauty and symmetry, he
stepped upon the speaker's stand, in these respects far in advance of
his compeers. His style of delivery was impressive, graceful and at
times impassioned, never rising to a scream or breaking into wild ges-
ticulations, and never descending into indistinctiveness or lassitude.
His style of composition was chaste, finished, flowing and beautiful,
often swelling up into rarest eloquence or melting down into the ten-
derest pathos. His prepared orations were completed with the severest
care. As the sculptor chisels down and finishes his statue, chipping
and chipping away the stone to find within his beautiful ideal, so did

he elaborate his thoughts till they assumed the shape he would give them, and so will retain them forever."

He died suddenly on September 4, 1859, and lies buried in Crown Hill Cemetery, Indianapolis.

Col. Abel C. Pepper, Indian Agent.

Col. Abel C. Pepper, the government Indian Agent, who then was stationed at Logansport, and who made the requisition for the company of militia ordered by Governor Wallace, was born in Shenandoah county, Virginia, in 1793, and died at Rising Sun, Indiana, March 20, 1860. He had filled numerous offices under the state and nation, always with entire acceptability. Especially did he render valuable services to his state in securing treaties with the Pottawattomie Indians in Northern Indiana by which the lands reserved for them by former treaties were ceded back to the government and opened to entry by the white settlers of that time. Between December, 1834 and September, 1836 he had, without assistance, concluded eight treaties for lands held by the Indians north of the Tippecanoe River, embracing about 80,000 acres. In all these treaties a provision was inserted that the Indians should remove within two years to the western reservation provided by the government. Me-no-mi-nee and his band refusing to go, Colonel Pepper made the requisition for the company of volunteer militia above referred to.

In all the walks of life Col. Pepper was an exemplary citizen. He lived respected, and died regretted by all who knew him.

Last Visit to the Indian Burial Ground.

On the day prior to the exodus a meeting of the Indians was held at the little grave yard, a short distance from the village, at which a final farewell of the dead was taken by those who were to leave the following morning never to return. Addresses were made by the chiefs present and by several white settlers. An address of some length was delivered by Myron H. Orton, of LaPorte, which was afterwards printed, but unfortunately no copies of it can now be found. The scene is said to have been affecting in the extreme. Weeping and wailing, which was confined to a few at first, became general, and until they were finally induced to disperse, it looked as though a riot would surely ensue. In solemn reverence they turned their weeping faces from the sleeping dead, never to look upon the graves of their kindred again.

Getting Ready to Move.

General Tipton recruited and organized the company of soldiers authorized by Governor Wallace within forty-eight hours after the requisition was made. These recruits were nearly all from Cass county, at Logansport, and in the vicinity. They started from Logansport the

COL. ABEL C. PEPPER.

The Government's Indian Agent, Stationed at Logansport, September, 1838.

latter part of August, marching along the Michigan Road through Rochester, across Tippecanoe River, and then along the old Indian trail north-westward, until they came to Me-no-mi-nee Village at Twin Lakes, five miles south-west from Plymouth. A great many of the white settlers in the neighborhood turned out to welcome the soldiers, and to render such assistance as might be necessary. The Indians were surrounded before they realized that the soldiers had been sent to remove them. They were disarmed, and preparations at once commenced for the starting of the caravan. Squads of soldiers were sent out in every direction for the purpose of capturing the straggling bands encamped in various places in the county, and such others as might be found hunting and fishing in the neighborhood. Several days were occupied in getting everything in readiness. The names of heads of families, and other Indians were registered, and when the list was completed it showed a total of 859. When all was in readiness to move, the wigwams and cabins were torn down and Me-no-mi-nee Village had the appearance of having been swept by a hurricane. Early on the morning of September 2, 1838 orders were given to move, and at once nearly one thousand men, women and children, with broken hearts and tearful eyes, took up the line of march to their far western home.

General Tipton's Report to Governor Wallace.

General Tipton accompanied the Indians as far as Sandusky Point, where he made the following report to Governor Wallace:

ENCAMPMENT, SANDUSKY POINT, ILLINOIS,
September 18, 1838.

DEAR SIR:—I have the honor to inform you that the volunteers under my command reached this place last evening with 859 Pottawattomie Indians. Three persons improperly called chiefs—Me-no-mi-nee, Black Wolf, and Pe-pin-a-wa—are of the number. I have this morning put the Indians under the charge of Judge Wm. Polke, who has been appointed by the United States to conduct them west of the Missouri River. I have also the honor to lay before your excellency a copy of my orderly book, or daily journal, to which I beg leave to refer a detailed statement of the manner in which my duties have been performed as commanding officer of volunteers engaged in this delicate service.

It may be the opinion of those not well informed upon the subject that the expedition was uncalled for, but I feel confident that nothing but the presence of an armed force for the protection of the citizens of the state and to punish the insolence of the Indians could have prevented bloodshed. The arrival of the volunteers in the Indian village was the first intimation they had of the movement of men with arms.

Many of the Indian men were assembled near the chapel when we arrived and were not permitted to leave camp or separate until matters were amicably settled, and they had agreed to give peaceable possession of the land sold by them. I did not feel authorized to drive these poor degraded beings from our state, but to remove them from the reserve, and to give peace and security to our citizens. But I found the Indians did not own an acre of land east of the Mississippi; that the government was bound to remove them to the Osage river, to support them one year after their arrival west, and to give to each individual of the tribe 320 acres of land. Most of them appeared willing to do so. Three of their principal men, however, expressed a wish to be governed by the advice of their priest, (Mr. Petit, a Catholic gentleman) who had resided with them up to the time of the commencement of the quarrel between the Indians and the whites, when he left Twin Lakes and retired to South Bend. I addressed a letter inviting him to join the emigration and go west. He has accepted the invitation and I am happy to inform you that he joined us two days ago, and is going west with the Indians. It is but justice to him to say that he has, both by example and precept, produced a very favorable change in the morals and industry of the Indians, that his untiring zeal in the cause of civilization has been, and will continue to be, eventually beneficial to these unfortunate Pottawattomies, when they reach their new abode. All are now satisfied and appear anxious to proceed on their journey to their new homes, where they anticipate peace, security and happiness. It may be expected that I should give your excellency an intimation or an opinion of the causes which have led up to the difficulty now happily terminated. A few words on that subject must suffice.

First the pernicious practice (I believe first introduced into our Indian treaty making at Fort Meigs in 1817) of making reservations of land to satisfy individual Indians, and sometimes white men, opened the door for both speculation and fraud.

By the treaty of 1832, the Pottawattomie Indians sold all their claims to land within the state of Indiana, except a few small reserves for particular tribes and parties. These reservations did not vest in the chief of any party a fee in the lands reserved; the original Indian title remained undisturbed, as you will see by the opinion of the Attorney General of the United States in the case of a reserve made by a treaty with the Prairie Pottawattomies October 20, 1832, to which I beg leave to refer. Me-no-mi-nee Reserve, about which the dispute originated, was made for his band by the treaty of 1832; he being a principal man (but not a chief) was first named, and the reserve has ever since been called by both Indians and white men "Me-no-mi-nee's Reserve." In 1834 a commissioner was appointed by the President to purchase that reservation. He succeeded in purchasing one-half the land at 50 cents per acre; the other half (11 sections) was reserved for individual Indians and whites, Me-no-mi-nee coming in for a large share of individual property. Hence the other Indians would have been defrauded out of their just claim to an interest in the reserve if that treaty had been confirmed. But the President, viewing the matter in the true light, did not submit the treaty to the Senate, but appointed A. C. Pepper, and authorized him to open the negotiation and purchase all the land for the government. He succeeded in purchasing the whole of the reserve at $1 per acre. Me-no-mi-nee did not sign the latter treaty, because he could not possess himself of a moiety of the land, and endow the chapel with the balance. By the treaty of 1836 the Indians reserved the right to remain on the lands for two years. The time expired on the 5th of that month (August, 1838) and the Indians refused to give possession to the settlers who had entered upon the land in anticipation of the passage of the pre-emption law. The passage of the law of June 22nd last gave to each settler who had resided on the reserve for four months previous to that day, a pre-emption right to 160 acres of land. On the 5th of last month, the day on which the Indians were to have left the reservation, the whites demanded possession, which they— the Indians—absolutely refused. Quarrels ensued and between the 15th and 20th the Indians chopped the door of one of the settlers, Mr. Watters, and threatened his life (see his certificate marked A.). This was followed by the burning of ten or twelve Indian cabins which produced a state of feeling bordering on hostilities. The assistant superintendant of emigration who had been stationed in the vicinity for some months, had failed to get up an emigrating party, and the public interpreters were so much alarmed as to be unwilling to remain in the Indian villages. I entertain no doubt but for the steps taken by your excellency, murders would have been committed on both sides in a sew days. The arrival of an armed force sufficient to put down the hostile movement against our citizens effected in three days what counseling and fair words had failed to do in as many months.

I see no reason for censuring the officers to whose charge the emigration has been confided. They should, perhaps, have prevented the Indians from planting corn in June when every one must have known that they would be ousted on the 5th of August. But on the other hand the Indians had the right of possession until August 5th, 1838. The Indians were under the influence of bad counsel from different sources. They were owing large debts to the traders who opposed the emigration of the Indians before their debts were paid or secured. Some were anxious to keep them where they were, hoping to obtain with ease a part of the money paid them as annuity. Lawyers, I am told, advised Me-no-mi-nee to keep possession and defend his claim to the reserve in our courts. Another class of men, both subtle and vigilant office-seekers, were using their influence to procure the dismissal of the officers heretofore engaged in the attempt to remove the Indians that they might succeed to the places of the present incumbents. And still another class, perhaps less wicked but not free from censure, is made up of those who influenced the Indians to plant corn and contend for the possession of the reserve. I am happy in being able to state that the removal of the Indians was effected without bloodshed or maltreatment. Every attention that could be was paid to their health, comfort and convenience. When on our marches, which are sometimes very much hurried, owing to the great distance between watering places, it is not unusual to see a number of volunteers walking whilst their horses are ridden by the sickly or infirm Indians. I found no difficulty in raising the number of volunteers required, although the people of the northern part of the state are much afflicted with sickness. I was compelled to discharge one or more every day and permit them to return home on account of bad health. The greatest number in service at any time was 97. The conductor of the emigration has requested me to place at his disposal 15 volunteers to attend the party, and keep order in the camp at night. Believing it necessary I have consented to do so, and have detailed Ensign B. H. Smith with 14 dragoons on the service. The rest of the corps will be discharged tomorrow.

In closing this report, already much longer than I could wish, I beg leave to express the obligation I am under to our mutual friend, Col. Bryant, who acted in the capacity of aid de camp, and has proved himself to be an excellent officer. I am not less indebted to Major Evans, of LaPorte. His knowledge of military discipline enabled him to be eminently useful. To Gen. N. D. Grover, Captains Hannegan and Holman, and Lieutenants Eldridge, LaSalle, Nash and Linton, and Ensigns McClure, Wilson, Smith and Holman, and to J. T. Douglass, adjutant, I am also under great obligations. Every commissioned officer and soldier has fully sustained the high character of western volunteers. I have the honor to be

Your Obedient Servant,

JOHN TIPTON.

P. S.— I transmit herewith for the information of your excellency an exhibit (B), showing the names of the Pottawattomie Indians as emigrants, and the number of their respective families.

General Tipton's Daily Journal.

The following is abridged from Gen. Tipton's daily journal of the occurrences that took place on the way:

TUESDAY, September 4th, 1838.— Left Twin Lakes, Marshall County, Indiana, early this morning. Traveling today was attended with much distress on account of the scarcity of water. Provisions and forage were also very scarce and of poor quality. The distance made was 21 miles.

CHIP-PE-WAY VILLAGE.

Camping Ground First Night at Time of Removal, September 2nd, 1838:
On Tippecanoe River at the Crossing of Michigan Road, Three Miles North
of Rochester.

WEDNESDAY. 5th.—Fifty-one persons were found to be unable to continue the journey on account of the want of transportation and were left, the most of them sick, with some to care for them. On account of the difficulty of finding water, a distance of only 9 miles was traveled. On the evening of this day a child died and was buried the next morning.

THURSDAY, 6th.—A distance of 17 miles was traveled and less of suffering and difficulty was experienced than on either of the previous days. During the evening 9 persons left behind the day before came into camp.

FRIDAY, 7th.—Thirteen persons more of the number left on Wednesday came into camp. Eighteen persons belonging to different families also joined the expedition. A child died in the morning.

SATURDAY, 8th.—A child 3 years old died and was buried. A chief, named We-wis-sa, came in with his family consisting of 6 persons. Two wagons which had been sent back for those left behind at Chippeway on Wednesday, returned bringing 22 person, the whole number left behind, except 9 who were unable to travel, and a few who had managed to escape. It was arranged for those left behind to be taken care of until able to proceed on the way.

SUNDAY, 9th. Physicians came into camp and reported about 300 cases of sickness which they pronounced of a temporary character. A kind of hospital was erected to facilitate the administering of medical treatment. Two children died this day.

MONDAY, 10th —The journey was renewed and 21 persons inclusive of sick and their attendants were left behind. The day was hot, but as the journey was made along the Wabash, there was not so much suffering for water. On the evening and night after getting into camp a child and man died.

TUESDAY, 11th.—A distance of 17 miles was accomplished through an open and champaign country with only the difficulties of procuring subsistance and forage.

WEDNESDAY, 12th.—The distance traveled from camp to camp was fifteen miles. The encampment was made near Tippecanoe Battle Ground. At this place a quantity of dry goods, such as cloaks, blankets, calicoes, etc., amounting to $5,469.81 was distributed among the Indians. Here, too, a very old woman, the mother of We-wis-sa, died. She was said to be over 100 years old.

THURSDAY, 13th.—A distance of eighteen miles was traveled. The sultry heat and the dust were the chief drawbacks on the way. Two physicians were called in to prescribe for those indisposed. They reported a hundred and sixty cases of sickness.

FRIDAY, 14th.—A journey of eighteen miles was made over a dry and unhealthy portion of the country. Persons who through weariness and fatigue were continually falling sick along the route and the wagons to transport them were becoming daily more and more crowded. As the party advanced into the prairies the streams were found to be literally dried up. Two deaths took place on the evening of this day.

SATURDAY, 15th.—After traveling ten miles the migrating party were forced to encamp at noon near an unhealthy and filthy looking stream as it was learned that there would be no chance of a better place that day. Two small children died along the road.

SUNDAY, 16th.—Danville in Illinois was reached after a journey of fifteen miles, a large part of the way being over the Grand Prairie. The heat and the dust made the traveling distressing. In the morning several persons were left sick in camp. The horses had become jaded, the Indians sickly, and many persons engaged in the emigration more or less sick. The whole country passed through was afflicted, as every village and hamlet had its invalids. Provisions and forage were found more enormously dear the farther the advance of the party. The sickness of the whole country was found to be unparalleled. Four persons in the little town near the encampment had died the day before.

MONDAY, 17th.—The volunteers and 859 Pottawattomie Indians reached Sandusky Point where they were turned over to Judge William Polke to conduct them west of the Mississippi river.

Of the onward journey under the management of Judge Polke we have only the general statement that 150 persons were lost on the whole way by death and desertion. What amount of suffering fell to the lot of these poor Indians every day on this horrible journey! Hundreds of them were daily burning with the terrible malarious fever so universally prevalent during the warm part of 1838. These hundreds were crowded into common rough wagons and compelled to bear the downpouring rays of a sultry sun and the only beverage to quench the prevailing thirst dipped from some mud stream just drying up. The food was composed of beef and flour cooked as might be while encamped for the night. Alas, how these poor little dusky infants must have suffered! No wonder that their little graves marked the daily journeys!

General John Tipton.

Gen. John Tipton, who figured so conspicuously in the removal of the Indians, had previously taken a very active part in protecting the early pioneers from Indian depredations on the frontiers, and especially in the battle of Tippecanoe against the Shawnees.

He was born in Sevier county, Tennessee, August 14, 1786. While young he moved with his parents to the west where his father became a leader in the defense of the frontier against the hostile Indians and was murdered by the savages in 1793. Left fatherless and on his own

GENERAL JOHN TIPTON.

Commander of the Soldiers at the Removal of the Indians from Twin Lakes, Marshall County, September 2, 1838.

resources, in the fall of 1807, with his mother, two sisters, and a half brother, he removed to the then Indiana territory, and settled on the Ohio river.　In June, 1807, he enlisted in a company recruited in his neighborhood, which was soon afterwards ordered to the frontier for the protection of settlements.

In September, 1811, the company entered the campaign which terminated in the battle of Tippecanoe, November 7, 1811.　Early in that memorable engagement all of Major Tipton's superior officers were killed, and he was promoted to the captaincy when the conflict was at its height.　He kept a journal of the campaign which is still in existence.　It is written on common writing paper, folded and stitched, and is yellow with age.　At that time he had received very little education, and was quite illiterate.　His account of the battle and the events that occurred about that time is given as it appears in his journal, spelling and all, as follows:

"Wednesday the 6 a verry Cold day.　We moved early a scout sent out they Came back and seed indian sines.　We march as usel till 12 Our spies caught four horses and seed some indians.　Stopt in a prairie the foot throwed all their napsacks in the waggons.　we formed in order for Battle—marched 2 miles then formed the line of Battle we marched in 5 lines on the extreme Right.　went into a cornfield then up to the above town and surrounded it they met us Pled for Peace they Said they would give us Satisfaction in the morning.　All the time we ware there they kept hollowing.　This town is on the west side of wabash — miles above Vincinnis on the Second Bank neat built about 2 hundred yards from the river.　This is the main town, but it is scattering a mile long all the way a fine cornfield, after the above moovment we mooved one mile farther up.　Camped in timber between a Creek and Prairie after crossing a fine creek and marching 11 miles.

"Thursday the 7 agreeble to their promisd.　Last night we were answered by the firing of guns and the Shawnies Breaking into our Tents a blood combat Took Place at precisely 15 minutes before 5 in the morning which lasted two hours and 20 minutes of a continewel firing white many times mixed among the indians so that we Could not tell the indians and our men apart.　they kept up a firing on three sides of us took our tent from the gueard fire.　Our men fought Brave and by the timely help of Capt. Cook with a company of infantry we maid a charge and drove them out of the timber across the parairie.　Our Loost in killed and wounded was 179 and theirs greater than hours.　Among the dead was our Capt Spier Spencer and first Lieutenant Mcmahan and Capt Berry that had been attached to our company and 5 more killed Dead and 15 wounded.　after the indians gave ground we Burried our Dead.　Among the Kentuckians Was Killed Mayj. Owen, and Mayj Davis badly wounded and a number of others, in all killed and wounded was 179, but no company suffered like ours. We then held an election for officers I was elected captain.   we then built Breastworks our men in much confusion, our flower been too small and our beeve lost.   Last night onley half rations of whiskey and no corn for our horses.   my horse killed I got mcmahans to Ride.   37 of them had been killed wounded and lost last night.   I had one quart of whiskey.

"Friday the 8th a Cloudy day and last night was also wet and cold. we lay all night at our Breastwork fire in the morning Spies sent out found the indians had left their town, the horsemen was all sent to burn the town.   We went and found a Great Deal of Corn and some Dead indians in the houses. loaded 6 waggons with Corn and Burnt what was Estimated at 2 thousand bushels and 9 of our men died last night."

He soon with his companions returned to his home in Corydon, Indiana.   Subsequently he was, by regular gradation, promoted to the rank of Brigadier General, and given command of the militia in Southern Indiana.

He held numerous offices in county and state, always with honor and credit to himself.   He was a member of the legislature in 1819 and was chairman of the committee which selected and located the present capital of Indiana at Indianapolis.   In 1823 he was appointed General Agent for the Pottawattomie Indians on the Upper Wabash, Tippecanoe and Yellow Rivers, and established the agency at Fort Wayne, which was afterwards removed to Logansport.

At the session of the Legislature in 1831 he was elected United States Senator to fill the vacancy occasioned by the death of James Noble, and was elected in 1833 for the term ending in 1839.   He died on the morning of April 5, 1839, in the meridian of life, honored and respected by all who admired an honest, upright, conscientious citizen, neighbor and friend.

The Pottawattomie Mills.

The Pottawattomie Mill, provided by the third article of the treaty of October 16, 1826, was erected on the north-west shore of Lake Man-a-tou a short distance east of Rochester, and almost in sight of the spot where the Indians were camped on Tippecanoe river the first night after Gen. Tipton started them from Twin Lakes on their removal west of the Mississippi.

By a treaty made March 16, 1835, the Indians ceded all their lands in that part of Indiana, including the mill, and the miller provided for was no longer to be supported by the United States   The Indians, by the terms of the treaty, agreed to remove to the West within two years. Among the most noted chiefs who figured extensively here about that time was Au-be-nau-be.   By the terms of the treaty of January 21,

POTTAWATTOMIE MILL DAM.

Present Appearance of the Old Pottawattomie Mill Dam on the Outlet of Lake Manatou, near Rochester; Built in 1826.

JONATHAN JENNINGS.

First Governor of Indiana; Died July 26, 1834.

1833, he and his band were given thirty-two sections of land, which included his village that stood near Leiter's Ford. Aubenaube Township in Fulton County is named in his honor. Au-be-nau-be was not a very good Indian. He was nearly always drunk and quarrelsome. In one of his drunken sprees he killed one of his wives. Some time afterwards he was killed by his son, Pau-koo-shuk, in a log house later owned by Mr. Blodgett, west of the Michigan road, near the north Fulton county line. His band went peaceably to the Western Reservation about 1837.

An Anecdote of Au-be-nau-be.

In the negotiation of the treaty of October 26, 1832, an anecdote is told of Au-be-nau-be. (spelled Obanoby in that treaty) which will bear repeating here, as that old chief was one of the most important factors among the Pottawattome Indians in Northern Indiana at that time.

President Jackson appointed Gov. Jonathan Jennings a Commissioner to negotiate a treaty with the Indians of Northern Indiana. His associates on the commission were John W. Davis and Marks Crume, the treaty being held at the forks of the Wabash where the city of Huntington now stands, October 26, 1832. One who was present tells the story of what happened there as follows:

"During the preliminary council, Dr. John W. Davis, who was a pompous, big-feeling man, said something that gave offense to Obanoby one of the head chiefs of the Pottawattomies. Obanoby addressed Gov. Jennings, saying: 'Does our great father intend to insult us by sending such men to treat with us? Why did he not send Generals Cass and Tipton? You (pointing to Governor Jennings) good man and know how to treat us (Pointing to Crume)—He chipped beef for the squaws at Wabash;'—meaning that Crume was the beef contractor at the treaty of 1826. Then pointing to Dr. Davis he said: 'Big man and damn-fool.' The chief then spoke a few words to the Pottawattomies present, who gave one of their peculiar yells and left the council-house, and could only be induced to return after several days, and then only through the great influence of Governor Jennings. The signing of this treaty was the last official act of Governor Jennings.

Governor Jonathan Jennings.

Jonathan Jennings, first governor of Indiana was, probably, the most distinguished man, in many ways, who took an active part in the formation of the Indiana Territory, and later the organization of the State in 1816 He was born in Hunterdon county, New Jersey, in 1784. In his early days he studied law in Pennsylvania, but before being admitted to practice, he took passage at Pittsburg on a flat-boat, and floated down the river to Jeffersonville, where he landed, having deter-

mined to make that town his home.   Here he completed the study of
law and become a practitioner in the courts of that and other towns in
the territory.   He was subsequently made clerk of the territorial legislature, and while discharging the duties of that position, became a can-
didate for congress against Thomas Randolph, attorney of the territory.
He was elected by a small majority; was re-elected over Waller Taylor in 1811, and in 1813 chosen for the third time.   Early in 1816 he
reported a bill to Congress to enable the people of the territory to take
the necessary steps to convert it into a state.   Delegates to a convention
to form a state constitution were selected in May 1816, Gov. Jennings
being chosen one from the county of Clark.   When the convention
assembled he was honored by being chosen to preside over its delibera-
tions, and at the election which followed was elected governor of the
new state by a majority of 1277 votes over the territorial governor, Mr.
Posey, his opponent.   In this office he served six years, also acting as
Indian Commissioner in 1818 by appointment of President Monroe, and
again by appointment of President Jackson in 1832.   At the close of
his term as Governor he was elected representative in Congress for four
consecutive terms.   On leaving Congress he retired to his farm near
Charlestown, where he remained cultivating the soil and spending his
leisure time in his library until July 26, 1834, when the end came.   He
died at home surrounded by his family and friends, beloved by all.

He was a man of polished manners; one more fascinating would be
hard to find.   He was always gentle and kind to those about him.   He
was not an orator, but he could tell what he knew in a pleasing way.
He wrote well—perhaps as well as any of his successors in the Govern-
or's office.   He was an ambitious man, but his ambition was in the
right direction—to serve the people the best he could.   He had blue
eyes, fair complexion and sandy hair.   He was about five feet, e'ght and
one-half inches high, and in his latter days was inclined to corpulency.
He was broad shouldered and heavy set, and weighed about 180.   He
died comparatively young, but he did as much for the well-being of
Indiana as any man that ever lived.

The Pokagon Pottawattomie Village.

The Pokagon Pottawattomie Village, one of the earliest Indian villages in Northern Indiana, and where many of the most stirring scenes
occurred prior to the removal of the Indians to the western country
provided for them, was located on the line between Indiana and Michigan, north of South Bend and about one mile west of the St.
Joseph river.

Leopold Po-ka-gon, the elder, was the second in rank among the
chiefs of his tribe, To-pin-a-be being the first.   Pokagon and his people were noted as being the farthest advanced in civilization of all their

SIMON POKAGON.

Distinguished Pottawattomie Indian. Born at Pokagon Village in 1830; Died at his home near Hartford, Michigan, January 25, 1899.

race in the St. Joseph Valley. He has been described as a man of considerable talents, and in his many business transactions with the early settlers was never known to break his word. He set a good example to his followers by not indulging in "fire water" (whisky). He was particularly distinguished for his devotion to the traditional teachings of the Jesuit Fathers. After the destruction of Ft St. Joseph by the Spaniards in 1781, says Mr. Leeper in "Some Early Local Foot Prints," the St. Joseph Valley was practically abandoned as a missionary field for nearly a half century. Pokagon made several visits to Detroit especially to ask that the black gowns (missionaries) be again sent among his people. The last of these appeals was July, 1830. Detroit was then the residence of M. Gabriel Richard, vicar general of the bishop of Cincinnati, and to the church official Pokagon poured out the deep yearnings of his soul. "Father, Father," he exclaimed, "I come to beg you to send us a black gown to teach us the word of God. We are ready to give up whisky and all our barbarous customs. Thou dost not send us a black gown and thou hast often promised us one. What! Must we live and die in our ignorance? If thou hast no pity on us, take pity on our poor children, who will live as we have lived, in ignorance and vice." And he went on to recount how his people had preserved the prayers taught their ancestors by the black gown formerly at St. Joseph; how his wife and children, every night and morning, prayed before the crucifix; how the men, women and children of his band fasted according to the traditions of their fathers and mothers. M. Frederick Reze was sent temporarily to minister to these urgent spiritual demands. July 22, 1830 he began his work baptizing Pokagon and his wife, respectively as Leopold and Elizabeth; the one at 55 and the other at 46. Pokagon died in Cass County, Michigan about 1841.

Simon Pokagon.

Simon Pokagon, a distinguished Pottawattomie Indian still living near Hartford, Michigan, is the only living son of Leopold Pokagon, having been born at Pokagon Village in 1830. He has the distinction of being the best educated and most distinguished full blooded Indian, probably, in America. He has written much and delivered many addresses of real literary merit during the past quarter of a century, and when he passes away he will leave no successor in this line worthy of the name. He has managed the band of about 200, of which he has for many years been the acknowledged head, with consummate skill and ability, and while the band, of which he is the most prominent member, have not made much headway in keeping pace with the rapid advance of civilization the past fifty years, yet had it not been for Pokagon, his education, enlightened views, and influence exerted in the right direction, it is likely they would have retrograded, disintegrated, and would undoubtedly long since have been scattered to the four winds of heaven. While the old chief has his faults, "even as you and I," yet when his history comes to be written in the years to come, he will be accorded the highest round on the ladder of fame among the great men of the once powerful tribe of Pottawattomie Indians.

Menominee Village.

Menominee village, where the Indians were surrounded and made prisoners by the soldiers under command of General Tipton, was a short distance north of Twin Lakes (called by the Indians Chi-chi-pe Ou-ti-pe) in Marshall County. The burial ground was located a short distance north-west of the village. The Indian chapel was situated on the north bank of the middle Twin Lake about twenty rods west of the Vandalia rail road. The chapel was erected by Rev. Stephen Theodore Badin, the first Catholic priest ordained in the United States. He was born at Orleans, France, in 1768, ordained May 23, 1793, and died at Cincinnati April 19, 1853. He had not long before erected a chapel at Pokagon Village north of South Bend, a short distance north of the line between Indiana and Michigan. The Twin Lakes chapel was erected about 1830, and was built of hewn logs, and covered with clap-boards. It was about 20x30 feet, the west half being two stories high. There was a hall-way through the center. The room for the missionary was over the west end of the chapel, and it was reached from below by means of a rustic ladder. The furniture was of the most primitive kind, and the food corn and wild meat and such fruits and vegetables as were suitable to eat during the summer season. This chapel, it is much to be regretted, was torn down many years ago. The spot where it stood is, however, plainly visible.

Ministrations of Father De Seille.

Father Badin was succeeded as missionary at the chapel by Father De Seille, probably about 1832-3, and continued until about 1837. He is described as a man of grave and reserved manner. His long intercourse with the Indians imparted to him a tinge of their own deep melancholy. His face, though youthful, bore the traces of suffering and the marks of tears; abstinence was written on his brow and his downcast eye accorded with his meek profession. But under that calm exterior beat the burning heart of an apostle whose every breath was for God. The love of the Indians for him was beyond expression; they loved him as their father, benefactor and friend; as "the good messenger of the good God."

Bishop Brute, of Vincennes, visited Northern Indiana in 1836, and describes the missions of Father DeSeille as follows: "A large number of their huts are built around the chapel, which is constructed of bark,

REV. STEPHEN THEODORE BADIN.

Born at Orleans, France, in 1760; Ordained May 23, 1793; Died at Cincinnati, April 19, 1853; First Catholic Priest Ordained in the United States.

with a cross erected behind and rising above it, and filled with rudely-made benches. The Indians begin and end their work without hammer, saw or nails, the ax being their only implement, and bits of skin or bark serving to fasten the pieces together. The room of the missionary is over the chapel, the floor of the one forming the ceiling of the other. A ladder in the corner leads to it, and his furniture consists, as did the prophets, of a table and chair, and a bed, or rather a hammock swung on ropes. Around the room are his books, and the trunks which contain the articles used in his chapel, as well as his own apparel. He spends his life with his good people, sharing their corn and meat, with water for his drink, and tea made from the herbs of his little garden. He abjures all spirits, as all Catholic Indians are forbidden to touch that which is the bane of their race, and he would encourage them with his example. I attended at the evening catechism, prayers and canticles, and in the morning said mass, at which a large number attended."

Father Benjamin Marie Petit.

Father Benjamin Marie Petit succeeded Father DeSeille about 1837-8, his first record appearing March 25, 1838. This ardent youthful spirit evinced an intense enthusiasm from first to last in the work of his chosen field, and in an outburst of fervency he tells something of his feelings and of his ministrations. " How I love these children of mine," he exclaimed, " and what pleasure it is for me to find myself amongst them. There are now from 1,000 to 1,200 Christians. Could you see the little children when I enter a cabin crowding around me and climbing on my knees—the father and mother making the sign of the cross in pious recollection, and then coming with a confiding smile on their faces to shake hands with me—you could not but love them as I do." And again: " When I am traveling in the woods, if I perceive an Indian hut, or even an abandoned encampment, I find my heart beat with joy. If I discover any Indians on my road, all my fatigue is forgotten, and when their smiles greet me at a distance, I feel as if I were in the midst of my own family." This was at Twin Lakes, Marshall county, Indiana, then known as " Chi-chi-pe Ou-ti-pe."

Of the chapel exercises he gives the following interesting account: " At sunrise the first peal was rung; then you might see the savages moving along the paths of the forest and the borders of the lakes; when they were assembled the second peal was rung. The catechist then in an animated manner gave the substance of the sermon preached the evening before; a chapter of the catechism was read and morning prayers were recited. I then said mass, the congregation singing hymns the while; after which I preached, my sermon being translated as I proceeded by a respectable French lady, 72 years old, who has devoted herself to the missions in the capacity of interpreter. The sermon was followed by a pater and an ave; after which the congregation sang a hymn to Our Lady, and quietly dispersed. The next thing was confession, which lasted till evening, and sometimes was resumed after supper. At sunset the natives again assembled for catechism, followed by an exhortation and evening prayers, which finished with a hymn to Our Lady. I then gave them my benediction—the benediction of poor Benjamin! Many practice frequent communion." In the first three weeks of his pastorate he baptized eighteen adults and blessed nine marriages.

But all this while a heavy grief lay at his heart. He knew that his joy was to be short lived; that his "dear Indians" were soon to be taken from him and banished to the far West. In the bitter anguish of his soul he exclaimed: "I shall have to level the altar and church to the ground, and bury the cross which overshadows the tombs to save them from profanation. And those Christian souls will pine away, deprived of those sacraments which they approached with so much fervor, and languishing under an unknown sky where I, their father, shall be unable to follow them."

Characteristics of Father Petit.

From a sketch of the Catholic Missionaries of Northern Indiana, published in *Are Maria* many years ago, the following in regard to Father Petit, will be of special interest in this connection:

"All agree in saying that an indefatigable and burning zeal never was seen under more amiable and graceful form, than in Rev. Father Petit. We never knew him, but after repeatedly visiting his admirable mother and brothers in Rennes, we readily formed an idea of the lovely and winning qualities of the dear departed missionary.

"He had literally become a sort of idol among his beloved savages, whose frankness and childlike simplicity delighted him. In writing of them, his style reveals a freshness of sentiment, of gladness and love almost without parallel. In 1838 he writes as follows: "Here I am in my Indian Church of Chi-chi-pe Ou-ti-pe. [This was the Indian Chapel at Twin Lakes.] How I love my children and delight in being among them! The fervor and simplicity that reigns among them is most touching and admirable. On New Year's eve I was asleep on my mat when the loud report of musketry made me spring up, wide awake; it is easy to make one's toilet when one sleeps on a mat. I ran to my door, when in rushed a troop of Indians—men, women and children—who, kneeling around me, begged my blessing for the New Year. Then with happy smiles they all came forward to shake hands. It was truly a family festival.

"Now my cherished place of residence is in my Indian village [Menominee village]; here I have a grand habitation, built of entire logs, placed one above the other; in more than one place we can see daylight through the walls. My fireplace is large enough to contain a quarter of a cord of wood. I have no carpet, and the boards of my floor are so slightly fastened that they yield to the pressure of the foot, like the keys of the piano to the musicians fingers."

Again he writes: "The nomadic life of the missionary is calculated to disengage his affections from the earth. In going so constantly from place to place, one feels that life is but a passing journey. Never before did I feel such entire liberty of heart. I think I can say with truth that I desire to die, if it pleases the Lord, without, however, experiencing any of the fatigues of life. It seems to me that in the midst of these labors, my health grows stronger. So be it; perhaps forty years of missionary duties and then Heaven; perhaps forty days and then Heaven! It matters but little. I am satisfied with either provided I am well with God."

But he had soon the sad prospect of seeing his Indian mission destroyed. The governor of Indiana had ordered troops to be raised to remove by force the Indians under his charge at Twin Lakes to the reservation west of the Mississippi. On this occasion he writes: "If my poor congregations must go into exile, I shall have to destroy the altar and church, and take the crosses from the graves in order that they may not be desecrated by heretical hands. What will these Christian souls do in the far west, without the aid of the Sacraments? I, their Father, in all probability, will not be able to accompany them, although I shall do all in my power not to abandon them."

On May 31st, 1838, he again wrote: "It is long since I have written you, but during the Easter times the poor missionary is overwhelmed with work. I had to give the Paschal exercises at Bertrand, Michigan, then at South Bend, then to my Indian congregation at Chi-chi-pe Outi-pe [Twin Lakes] twenty-five miles distant, where for five weeks I heard confessions from morning until night without any repose, except two visits to the sick who lived forty miles apart. From Chi-chi-pe I had to carry the consolations of religion to the chief, Pokagon, who lived at a distance of sixty miles. [In Michigan, west of the St. Joseph river and north of South Bend.] You may perhaps think that missionaries are saints, but I must tell you that during all that time I was unable to pray to God, for as soon as the confessions were finished and my breviary said, I fell asleep upon my mat. My sleep, at least, is always good, calm, gentle and undisturbed, as an infant's. It is true, and this thought consoles me, the labor and fatigue of the day were all for the glory of the Good Master, to whom I give myself without reserve. May He accept it as a continual prayer; it is, for those who know how to offer it, a continual

sacrifice. Nevertheless, there are moments when the heart seems ready
to burst with joy and the eyes overflow with sweet tears. Oh, it is so
good to feel that one has nothing to do in the world but work for God.
Thanks, thanks, my God."

About this time the government sent officers to arrange for the departure of the Indians. Father Petit again writes:

"One morning I said mass, and immediately afterward we began removing all the ornaments from my dear little church. At the moment
of my departure I asembled all my children to speak to them for the
last time. I wept, and my auditors sobbed aloud; it was indeed a heart-
rending sight, and over our dying mission we prayed for the success of
those they would establish in their new hunting grounds. We then
with one accord sang:

"O, Virgin, we place our confidence in Thee."

"It was often interrupted by sobs and but few voices were able to
finish it. I then left them. Oh, it was indeed sad for a missionary to
see a work so young and vigorous expire in his arms. Some days afterward I learned that the Indians, notwithstanding their peaceable dis-
positions, had been surprised and made prisoners of war, under pretence
of a council they were all reunited when the military force secured 400.
The government sent at the same time to invite me to accompany
them to their new destination. It seems that their separation from
their pastor was one of the motives which prevented the Indians from
consenting to go quietly to their exile. I replied that I could take no
steps without permission of my Bishop."

The order was given to march without further delay. The Indians
were driven on at the point of the bayonet; many were sick, huddled together in transport wagons; numbers died of heat and thirst.

It happened, however, that Bishop Brute was to consecrate a church
in a neighboring mission on the 9th of September; and on the 7th the
Indians would be encamped within a mile of the place. Two days before, the Bishop entered Father Petit's room. Together they set out
for Logansport and on their way learned of the sufferings of the poor
Indians. The news was like a dagger in the heart of Father Petit, but
to his delight the Bishop gave him permission to follow the emigrants
on condition of returning as soon as he was summoned; and he hasten-
ed immediately to his post.

No sooner did it get abroad that the priest was come than the whole
camp was in motion; the natives flocked out to meet him, the whites
drawn up in file formed a lane for him to pass. The enthusiasm was
unbounded and the officer in command said, "This man has more power

here than I have." On Sunday Father Petit said mass, and vespers were sung. On the 16th he rejoined his flock. He found them moving onward, enveloped in clouds of dust, and surrounded by the soldiers who hurried on their march. Behind came the wagons, in which were crowded together the sick, the women, and the children. The scene as described by Father Petit was one of the most mournful description; the children, overcome by heat, were reduced to a wretched state of languor and exhaustion. By this time the general had begun to understand something of Father Petit's worth, and treated him with marked respect. The chiefs who had hitherto been treated as prisoners of war were released at the priest's request and took their place with the rest of the tribe. First went the flag of the United States borne by a dragoon; after which came the baggage; then the vehicle occupied by the native chiefs; next followed the main body of the emigrants, men, women and children, mounted on horses, marching in file after Indian fashion, while all along the flanks of the multitude might be seen dragoons and volunteers urging on unwilling stragglers, often with the most violent words and gestures. The sick were in their wagons under an awning of canvas, which, however, far from protecting them from the stifling heat and dust, only deprived them of air. The interior was like an oven and many consequently died. Six miles from Danville. Illinois, there was a halt for two days. "When we quitted the spot," he said, "we left six graves under the shadow of the cross." Order had been so thoroughly restored through the presence of the priest that the troops now retired, and Father Petit was left with the civil authorities to conduct the emigrants to their destination.

Having seen the emigrants safely landed—such as had not died and escaped on the way—Father Petit started on the return trip. At St. Louis he was taken sick from fatigue and malarial fever and died. His remains were afterward removed to Notre Dame, Indiana, where they lie buried in the Catholic cemetery at that place.

Sanford Cox Visits the Caravan.

Sanford C. Cox, of LaFayette, in his recollections of the "Early Settlement of the Wabash Valley," published in 1860, in speaking of this removal, says:

"Hearing that the large emigration, which consisted of about one thousand of all ages and sexes would pass within eight or nine miles west of LaFayette, a few of us procured horses and rode over to see the retiring band, as they reluctantly wended their way toward the setting sun. It was a sad and mournful spectacle to witness these children of the forest slowly retiring from the home of their childhood that contained not only the graves of their revered ancestors, but many endearing scenes to which their memories would ever recur as sunny spots along their pathway through the wilderness. They felt that they were bidding farewell to the hills, valleys and streams of their infancy. the more exciting hunting grounds of their advanced youth, as well as the stern and bloody battle-fields where they had contended in riper manhood—on which they had received wounds, and where many of their friends and loved relatives had fallen, covered with gore and with glory. All these they were leaving behind them to be desecrated by the plowshare of the white man. As they cast mournful glances backward toward these loved scenes that were rapidly fading in the distance, tears fell from the cheeks of the downcast warrior, old men trembled, matrons wept, the swarthy maiden cheek turned pale, and sighs and half-suppressed sobs escaped from the motly groups as they passed along. some on foot, some on horseback, and others in wagons—sad as a funeral procession. I saw several of the aged warriors casting glances toward the sky, as if they were imploring aid from the spirits of their departed heroes who were looking down upon them from the clouds, or from the great spirit who would ultimately redress the wrongs of the red man, whose broken bow had fallen from his hand, and whose sad heart was bleeding within him. Ever and anon one of the party would start back out into the bush and away to their old encampment. declaring that they would rather die than be banished from their country. Thus scores of discontented emigrants returned from different points on their journey, and it was several years before they could be induced to join their countrymen west of the Mississippi."

Me-no-mi-nee.

The Pottawattomie Indian, Me-no-mi-nee, was the central figure in the disturbances that lead to the raising of troops and the removal of the Indians by force from Twin Lakes, September 4, 1838. He was personally known to many of the original settlers of Marshall county, nearly all of whom, however, have long since passed away. In his history of Indian affairs, Rev. Isaac McCoy, a Baptist missionary, and the founder of Carey Mission, on the St. Joseph river, a short distance west of Niles, Michigan, thus speaks of Me-no-mi-nee, for whom the Menominee village was named. Writing from Ft. Wayne about 1821, he says:

"I had been informed by an Indian trader that on the Illinois river some hundred miles from Ft. Wayne, there was a company of religious Pu-ta-wat-o-mies, at the head of whom was one who was a kind of preacher, whose name was Menominee. As this man exhorted his followers to abstain from ardent spirits and many other vices, and to practice many good morals, and as a part of their religious services consisted in praying, I was induced to hope that their minds were somewhat prepared to receive religious instruction. My circumstances were such that I could not visit them at that time, but I wrote the leader a

MRS. ANGELINA SHIPSHEWANA.

Mrs. Angelina Shipshewana was a full-blood Pottawattomie Indian, and did not speak a word of English. She resided in the region of Cramstown, St. Joseph County, where she was born in the year 1821. Her history, like that of most of her race, was such as occurs in the lives of the children of the forest before the white man came.

letter to come to Ft. Wayne to see me, which he did about April 1st,
1821. He professed to have been called some few years previously by
the Great Spirit to preach to the Indians that they should forsake their
evil practices, among which he enumerated the vices of drunkenness,
theft, murder, and many other wicked practices. He had a few followers, the number of whom was increasing. Menominee appeared to be
more meek, and more ready to receive instruction than could have been
expected from a wild man who had arrogated to himself claims to be a
leader not only in temporal but also in spiritual things. At his particular request I gave him a writing in which I stated that he had been
several days with me, that I had heard him preach and pray, and had
conversed much with him; that I hoped his instructions would do his
people good, and therefore requested all to treat him with kindness.
" Now," said he, " I will go home and preach to my people all my life.
I will tell them that my father says I tell the truth."

Rev. Mr. McCoy Visits Me-no-mi-nee.

In June following, Rev. McCoy visited Menominee at his village
near Twin Lakes, in what is now Marshall County. It was then un-
organized territory. Of that visit he said: "As we approached the village, Menominee and others met us with all the signs of joy and gladness which could have been expressed by these poor creatures. Menominee immediately cried aloud to his people, all of whom [1821] lived
in four little bark huts, informing them that their father had arrived.
I was no sooner seated by their invitation than men, women and children came around and gave me their hand—even infants were brought,
that I might take them by the hand. A messenger was immediately
dispatched to a neighboring village to announce my arrival. In his
absence Menominee inquired if I had come to reside among them. Re-
ceiving evasive answers he expressed great concern. He said the principal chief of their party, and all the people of the villages, with few
exceptions desired me to come. He showed me a place which he had
selected for me to build a house upon. Their huts being exceedingly
hot and unpleasant, I proposed taking a seat out of doors. The yard
was immediately swept and mats spread for me to either sit or lie upon.
We were presently regaled with a bowl of boiled turtle's eggs; next
came a kettle of sweetened water for us to drink. I was then shown a
large turtle which had been taken in a pond, and asked if I were fond
of it. Fearing that with their cooking I should not be able to eat it,
I replied that I was very fond of corn and beans. This I knew was
already over the fire. It was placed before us in one large wooden
bowl, and we ate it with wooden ladles. Menominee had two wives,
each of whom presented me with a bark box of sugar containing about
thirty pounds each.

" In a short time the principal chief, Pcheeko [Che kose?] and every man and almost every woman and child in his village, were at Menominee's, and all came and shook hands. On the arrival of Pcheeko we had resumed our station in the house, where I handed out my tobacco, and all smoked until the fumes and heat became almost insufferable, but mustered courage to remain as I supposed it would be impolite to leave the room at that time.

A Visit to Pcheeko.

" In compliance with an invitation from the principal chief of this band—Pcheeko—we paid him a visit on the 12th of June, 1821, accompanied by Menominee and several others. Pcheeko, to show his loyalty to the government, or rather as an expression of respect for me, had hoisted over his hut the American flag. A large kettle of hominy and venison was ready for us on our arrival. To my mess, beside some choice pieces, they added sugar. With the help of my knife, a wooden ladle, and a good appetite, I dispatched a reasonable meal, endeavoring at the same time to indulge in as few thoughts as possible about the cleanliness of the cooks. In private they intimated to my interpreter, Abraham, that they suspected me to be partial to Menominee. The lad replied that my mission was to them all. They said that they were glad to attend the preaching, for they were afraid Menominee did not know how to preach good. On this subject Abraham replied to them that my business was preaching, teaching school and instructing the Indians in mechanical trades and in agriculture; that Menominee being a preacher, also knew by experience that preachers received but little pay, and had but little to give away. I then informed them that I desired to address them solely on the subject of religion, and wished the women also to hear. They were called, but were ashamed to come into the house, it not being customary for women to mingle with the men when in a council, from which they could not distinguish this assembly. The females generally seated themselves outside of the house, near enough to hear. All listened attentively to the discourse, then retired about half an hour, which time the principal men employed in private conversation. When we reassembled they made the following reply:

"'Our Father, we are glad to see you and have you among us. We are convinced that you come among us from motives of charity. We believe that you know what to tell us, and that you tell us the truth. We are glad to hear that you are coming among us to live near us, and when you shall have arrived we will visit your house often and hear you speak of these good things."

The bowl of hominy was then passed around the company again; all smoked, shook hands, and parted in friendship. On leaving some of them gave their blessing. The benediction of one was as follows:

"May the Great Spirit preserve your energy and health and conduct you safely to your family, give success to your labors, and bring you back to us again."

Mr. McCoy remained two days. "During the time," he said, "Menominee delivered to his people a lecture. He had no ceremony, but commenced without even rising from his seat, and spoke with much energy.

Me-no-mi-nee Had Two Wives.

"A little after dark the company dispersed and all shook hands with me as they had done at meeting. When we were alone Menominee informed me that he had two wives. Some had said that if I had knowledge of this circumstance I would push him away from me." "I tell you," said he, "that you may know it. It is a common custom among our people, and often the younger sister of a wife claims it as a privilege to become a second wife that she to may have some one to provide meat for her. This is the case in regard to my two wives who are sisters. I did not know it was wrong to take a second wife; but if you say it is wrong, I will put one of them away." This I thought appeared like cutting off a hand or pulling out an eye, because it offended, and I therefore said I must think before I speak in regard to it.

Me-no-mi-nee as a Preacher.

"Menominee at one time showed me a square stick on which he had made a mark for every sermon he had preached. I then showed him in my journal the list of texts from which I had preached at different times, showing at the same time that what I had preached had been taken from such and such places in our good book. He immediately began counting his marks and mine in order to ascertain which of us had preached most frequently in the course of a year. Finding a considerable difference in my favor he pleaded his inferiority. He must now see all my books and papers, hear me read, notwithstanding he could not understand a word. I attempted to write in my journal, but he kept so close to me that I had to defer it. I retired into the bush to make some hasty notes with my pencil, but he followed, and in a few minutes was seen gazing at me.

"The weather being excessively hot and we being obliged to use water taken from a filthy pond, the flies exceedingly severe on our horses, and our situation in every respect being very unpleasant and unwholesome, Abraham, who was already sick insisted on our leaving. He said: "We stay here, I'm sure we die; our horses die too. Me no want to die here." Menominee called together all his people, of whom I took an affectionate leave after promising them that, if practicable, I would visit them again when the leaves began to fall. Menominee walked with us half a mile, begged a continuation of our friendship, declared that he would continue to please God and do right—and so we parted.

"Among these tribes we rarely saw the men laboring in the field. The cultivation of the field was almost universally esteemed the business of the women. On our return trip we passed a small field in which a company of men were also laboring. Men, women, and children, came running to meet us at the fence, and gave me the parting hand. I did not see among them a particle of either bread or meat, excepting a few pigeons which they had killed with sticks; some deer might have been taken but they were destitute of powder and lead, and had not anything with which to purchase these articles. Excepting roots and weeds their only food at this time consisted of corn and dried beans, of which their stock was exceedingly small."

What Became of Me-no-mi-nee.

It may be a query in the minds of many what finally became of the good preacher, Menominee. The twenty-two sections of land ceded to him and Pe-pin-a-wa, Na-ta-ka and Mak-a-taw-ma-ah, were never transferred to the government by Menominee, and were he living whatever interest he then had would still be his. The other chiefs who shared with him in the ownership received $14,080 for their interest, but Menominee refused to sign the treaty, and never transferred his interest either by treaty or sale to the government or others. He was placed under military surveillance at the time of the removal from Twin Lakes, in 1838, and guarded by soldiers on the 900 mile march to the Western reservation. He was at this time a man well along in years, and it is more than likely, as he was never heard of afterward, that he died of a broken heart. As to the other chiefs associated with him in the ownership of the reservation, the white traders cheated them out of the money received for their share before they were removed, and in the mixing up of the various bands in the caravan, they lost their identity and disappeared—but

Whither they went and how they fared,
Nobody knew and nobody cared.

Me-no-mi-nee Cruelly Treated.

In view of all the facts as revealed by a careful investigation, the conviction forces itself upon me that Menominee and his band were cruelly treated and badly misused. Governor Wallace had as much right to order the raising of a company of troops to go to Twin Lakes and drive away the white settlers that were interfering with Menominee and his followers as he had to arrest Menominee and drive him at the point of the bayonet from his home he had not surrendered. If he had signed the treaty ceding his lands to the government, agreeing to remove to the Western reservation and had refused to do so, then the case would have been different. He had as good a right to remain on his lands at Twin Lakes as had Joseph Waters and his white following, who seem to have been the real cause of the disturbance. As I look at it, the whole affair was cruel and inhuman, and partook more of savagery than the act of a civilized, enlightened and Christian people. The Indians were surrounded by the soldiers before they were aware that force was to be used in driving them away. They were disarmed of guns, tomahawks and bows and arrows; their wigwams and cabins were torn down and destroyed, and the old and decrepid, the lame, the halt and the blind, the women and children, were marched off by the soldiers like so many cattle to the slaughter. And when the record shows that the graves of 109 of the poor, helpless beings mark the pathway of that sad and solemn procession, I can not resist the conclusion that a cruel wrong was done, which time can not condone, and which can not be forgiven here or hereafter.

RECOLLECTIONS OF EARLY RESIDENTS.

The following interviews with residents of Marshall county who were present at the time of the removal, or who were conversant with the facts, will be of historic value in this connection:

What William Sluyter Remembers.

WILLIAM SLUYTER—" I lived near the Menominee village, which was just north of Twin Lakes, in Marshall county, and was present at the time the Indians were congregated there, September 3-4, 1838, to be removed to the western reservation. The village was composed of log huts and wigwams of poles covered with bark and matting, erected w'thout any system. There were 75 or 100 of these primitive dwellings. A grave yard in which their dead were buried was near by. They buried their dead mostly by splitting logs in the middle and digging a trough in one part of it, putting the dead in and closing it up. Some of them were put under ground, and some were set upright with poles placed around them.

" There were several hundred Indians there at the time and quite a number of soldiers--State militia, I think. Col. A. C. Pepper, I believe, was there in immediate charge, while, I understood, General Tipton was the chief of the removal. I think the caravan went in a southwesterly direction near the north end of Lake Muk-sen-cuck-ee, thence southwest of Logansport and so on down a few miles west of the Wabash river.

" I saw no ill treatment of the Indians so far as the government was concerned. There were, however, individual cases of bad treatment by some of those in authority. The soldiers disarmed the Indians, taking from them their guns, tomahawks, axes, bows and arrows, knives, etc., and placed them in wagons for transportation. There were plenty of wagons to carry all who were unable to walk, but not many would consent to get into the wagons, never having seen any vehicles of that kind and were afraid of them. They marched off single file, with a soldier at the head of about every forty or fifty. It was indeed a sad sight to see them leaving their homes and hunting grounds where many of them had lived all their lives, and going to a strange land concerning which they knew nothing. After they left, the wigwams were torn down and burned; eventually the old chapel which was used as a guard-house was torn down, and the little graveyard was finally plowed over and obliterated, and no trace of the village, the chapel, or the graveyard can now be found."

David How's Statement.

DAVID How:—"I was about ten years old when the Indians were removed. I was there with my father, Isaac How, who lived near by, the night before the caravan started. My father was one of the guards at the chapel in which Chief Me-no-mi-nee, who refused to go peaceably, was confined. I should think there were several hundred Indians there at the time and a hundred or more soldiers. When they left a soldier was placed at the head of about every thirty or forty Indians. The Indians were all disarmed. Wagons were provided for all who were unable to walk and others, but most of them disliked to ride in a government wagon and all walked that possibly could. The Indians were brought to the village from different parts of Northern Indiana and Southern Michigan by squads of soldiers, who forced them to leave their villages, and after selecting such articles as could be conveniently carried and would be of use on the way, they tore down and burned up the huts and wigwams, and marched them off to the general redezvous. My sympathies were always with the Indians, and think many of them were shamefully treated."

Thomas Houghton's Recollections.

THOMAS K. HOUGHTON.—"In 1838 I lived with my father on the Indian trail between the Ben-ak village in Tippecanoe township and the Me-no-mi-nee village where the Indians were congregated to get ready to be removed. I was not there at the time but it was about the only subject of conversation for many years and I heard considerable about it. One incident connected with the removal I remember distinctly. Nigo was a Miami Indian who afterwards lived in Marshall county and died in Plymouth about 1880. He was forced by the soldiers to go to the place of rendezvous. After the caravan had started he went to Gen. Pepper on the second day out and told him he was not a Pottawattomie and that he was not on the list of those that had agreed in the treaties to go west of the Missouri. Gen. Pepper examined the list and found that such was the case. He told Nigo that it would not be safe for him to attempt to leave the caravan then as if he did he might be shot by the guards. He told him that when they camped that night to come to his tent and he would see what could be done. Gen. Pepper's headquarters that night was in a log cabin that had been previously vacated. At dark Nigo was promptly on hand. Gen. Pepper told him to take his blanket and go into the loft above and to lie down and go to sleep and remain there until after the caravan had moved away the next morning when he could get up and go where he pleased. Nigo did as directed, and next morning started back through the woods to his wigwam north of Bourbon where he remained until a few years prior to his death when he removed to Plymouth where he died as stated."

John Lowery's Recollections.

JOHN LOWERY.—"I lived close by the Indian chapel which was located on the north bank of Twin Lakes a few rods west of where the railroad crosses the wagon road, and near where the Indians congregated in 1838 preparatory to being removed to a reservation west of the Mississippi. I was not there at the time, being absent in Laporte county. I talked with those who were there, and with some who went with the Indians part of the way.

"Gen. Tipton was the moving agent, had command of the militia, and had had much to do with the Indians for many years previous in this part of the country, having been employed by the government to secure treaties for the extinguishment of the Indian titles to their reservations. The Pottawattomies were peaceable and were always kindly treated by him. There was no occasion for cruel treatment on his part and I am satisfied none was offered to any of them unless they deserved it. The time specified in the treaties for the Indians to remove having passed, Gen. Tipton sent squads of militia to the several villages in this part of the state with directions to require the Indians to assemble at the chapel on a day named as a starting place.

"At the appointed time nearly all that were able to go met at the chapel where a council was held and arrangements made for the start the next day. The chapel hall was used for the meeting of the council. The building was made of hewn logs and its dimensions were about 40x20 feet. The doors were not locked; no handcuffs were used and no indignities were shown any of the Indians so far as I have been able to learn. They were told that the treaties signed by their chiefs required them to go west to the reservation provided for them within two years from the date of the treaties, and that time having expired, it was their duty to go peaceably. Many of the Indians protested that the treaties had been procured by fraud, and had not been signed by those having authority to sign them, and that was the reason they had not gone peaceably before. The treaties, however, having been ratified by the government, and the reservations having been made subject to entry there was nothing to be done but to remove the Indians. That was done as quietly and humanely as it was posssible under the circumstances. The country was new and unimproved, and in Northern Indiana an unbroken wilderness. There were no wagon roads then and the Indian trail was difficult of passage with wagons and packhorses. There were among the Indians many old men and women, and pappooses, and not a few sick and unable to go without being transported in wagons or on packhorses. This was the condition on that September morning in 1838 when over 800 Indians started on their long journey."

Statement of I. N. Clary, Wagoner.

Mr. I. N. Clary, of Lucerne, Cass County, Indiana, since deceased, being interviewed said: "I was a boy of twenty and went with the caravan as a teamster, driving a four-horse team. Gen. Morgan, of Rush county, was major general, and Wm. Polke lieutenant. Dr. Jeroloman, of Logansport, was the physician in charge. The Indians camped the first night on the Tippecanoe river and the third night at Horney's Run, north of Logansport. The caravan moved in wagons and on foot, the Indian men walking and hunting as they went. The number of wagons was sixty and the distance made each day was from seven to twenty miles. Stops for the night were made where water was plenty and all slept in tents and wagons. The Indians were well treated by the removing party and did not suffer for food or water. The caravan went west from Logansport and passed through Sagama town; crossed Sagama river, and forded the Illinois river near Danville, Illinois, and passed through Jacksonville and Springfield, Illinois. We crossed the Mississippi river at Alldan, Illinois, in an old shattered steamboat that was not safe to cross on, and it took us two days before we were all on the other side. The grand river was crossed near the mouth of the Missouri, and that river at or near Independence. We left the Indians at a point near the Osage river in Kansas, having been sixty days making the journey."

A Table of Removals.

Quite a number who had secreted themselves in various places in Northern Indiana, and others who for one reason or another were unable to go with the caravan above referred to, went peaceably, under the supervision of Alexis Coquillard, during the summer of 1840. What remained of the Pottawattomies who had not entered land and settled down to peaceful pursuits, were congregated at South Bend some time in the summer of 1851, and conducted from there to the Western reservation, also under the direction of Alexis Coquillard, who had been awarded the contract by the government at a price agreed upon, to remove the Indians.

In a report made to the Indian department in 1840, it appears that Gen H. Brady was instructed by the secretary of war on February 26, 1840, to assume the direction of the emigration of the remainder of the Pottawattomies. A party of 536 set out, and 526 were delivered October 6, 1840, to the sub-agent at the place of their destination, and on October 16, General Brady reported that 430 more had set out, and on the 3rd of November were moving to the southwest.

In a letter addressed to George W. Ewing, of Fort Wayne, who was interested with Coquillard and others in the contract for the removal of the Indians, May 19, 1853, the commissioner of Indian affairs reported the number of Pottawattomies and other tribes who emigrated west as follows:

YEAR	IN CHARGE OF	NO. IN PARTY
1833	L. H Sands	67
1833	James Kennedy	179
1834	William Gordon	199
1835	Captain Russell	712
1836	G. Kerchival	634
1837	G. W. Proffit	53
1837	L H. Sands	447
1838	I S. Berry	150
1838	William Polk (General Tipton)	756
1840	A. Coquillard	526
1840	Godfrey and Kerchival	430
1851	A. Coquillard and others	639
	Total	4792

A large number removed themselves not included in the above table. In 1836 upwards of 500 so removed of whom no roll was furnished. In 1837 a party of 842 was enrolled and reported to the department which probably included the self emigrants of 1836.

In 1847 a party of between 700 and 800 who were probably not enrolled, were removed by Alexis Coquillard. No mention is made of the removal by the war department, and the information in regard to it is obtained from the following persons who went with the caravan:

BENJAMIN COQUILLARD, South Bend—"I accompanied my uncle, Alexis Coquillard, when he removed the Indians west in 1847. I am positive of the date from its being the year of the Mexican war. There were between seven and eight hundred men, women, and children, and 16 wagons in the caravan. The Indians were gathered from about Columbia City, Huntington, Manchester, South Bend, Peru and Winamac. They were mostly Pottawattomie and Miamis; stragglers and deserters from the 1846 removal which my uncle conducted. The caravan started about 11 miles north of Peru, Indiana, and traveled a little north of west through Winamac and Ottowa I don't remember any of the other points. We traveled about 33 miles per day. There were no deaths or desertions. The Indians were treated well; were provided with tents and ponies and also had the privilege of riding in the wagons. They had plenty of food, such as flour, bacon, coffee, beans, sugar, molasses, etc. White flour was used exclusively. Alexis Coquillard, the younger, was business manager, whose duty it was to go in advance to select camping places, and warn the people of the towns not to sell liquor to the Indians. Fannie, Alexis Coquillard's wife, was the only woman in the company."

CHARLES H. FRENCH, South Bend.—"I went with the removal of 1847, which was under the direction of Alexis Coquillard. The Indians were collected at Columbia City, Huntington, Manchester, South Bend, Peru and Winamac. I lived then in Kosciusko county, where Ezekiel French, my father joined the party at that point. We crossed the Mississippi at Burlington, and the Missouri about four miles from Independence. We crossed both rivers in flat-boats. I don't remember any other points enroute. We reached our destination near St. Mary's Mission, Kansas, about September 1st, having been on the way about thirty (?) days. The Indians were treated well; had plenty of substantial food; tents to sleep in if they wanted to, and the privilege of riding in the wagons. Only a few had ponies, as they were rather poor. The Indians went willingly, and there was no loss by death or desertion. The only difficulty experienced was in going through towns, where, unless watched, the Indians would secure whiskey, to prevent which the utmost precaution was used. Mrs. Coquillard was the only white woman in the company."

OWEN J. LENTZ, South Bend.—" I drove team for Alexis Coquillard when he took the Indians west in 1851. We started from South Bend in June with forty Indians and got six hundred more about Fondulac, Wisconsin; we were about four months on the way. Our rendezvous was at Theresa, on Fox River, about twenty miles above Fondulac, where I helped to collect the Wisconsin Indians. No force was used.

" We buried six or seven Indians west of the Missouri River who had died of cholera There were no desertions. They were treated well; had plenty to eat, and tents to sleep in, such as wanted them. The route was ten miles north of Madison, Wisconsin. We crossed the Mississippi at Eagle Point, three miles above Dubuque, on a horse ferry, thence through Iowa City, and crossed the Missouri at Ft. Leavenworth on a rope ferry. We had about half a dozen teams when we left South Bend, and seventy teams when the whole caravan was made up. The Indians had about three hundred ponies of their own. They were permitted to ride in the wagons whenever they chose to do so. Samuel L. Cottrell was the captain; John Mack, secretary, and Alexis Coquillard (younger), commissary.

" The ladies of the party were Mrs. Coquillard, Mrs. Cottrell, Matilda Rouseau and Frances C., Maria, and Clarissa Sancomb. The Coquillards and Captain Cottrell usually went ahead to secure food, the camping place, and warn the people of the villages not to sell whiskey to the Indians. Frances C. Sancomb became the wife of Francis D. LaSalle, of Fort Wayne, now the widow of Edward Edwards. Maria Sancomb became the first wife of the late ex-county clerk, George W. Matthews."

M. H. SCOTT, of Danville, Ill., in regard to a removal that occurred in 1837, says: " The party who removed the Indians consisted of Louis H. Sands, John B. Durett and myself, the superintendent of the removal being Col. A. C. Pepper, of Rising Sun, Indiana, whose headquarters were at Logansport. We went from Logansport to the Indian village near South Bend, where we collected them. There were about five hundred removed, most of whom were under Chief To-pin-e-bee. We wished to remove Po-ka-gon and his tribe also, but he refused to go, and obtained permission from the government to remove his tribe to Saganaw, Michigan. We took the five hundred Indians to Chicago. Our instructions were to get them to Kansas if possible; otherwise to Council Bluffs. At a consultation held in Chicago, two hundred agreed to go to Kansas, and I took them there. Sands took the others to Council Bluffs. Several families of half-breeds were removed by us from Chicago. We had no military organization whatever."

REMOVAL OF THE MIAMIS.

In this connection it seems germain to the subject under consideration that a pause be made here to record briefly the removal of a small
band of Miami Indians from Peru, on the north bank of the Wabash
River in 1846, by Alexis Coquillard, referred to frequently in the foregoing sketches. The Miamis and Pottawattomies were closely allied,
having lived and intermingled by association and marriage to that extent
for a long period of time that they had become by ties of blood, and by
habits and tribal customs, practically one tribe in this part of the country.

The history of the removal of this band is gathered from a correspondence from one of the removing party to the South Bend Register,
in October, 1846, then published by the late Vice-President Schuyler
Colfax, and for which the writer is indebted to Hon. D. R. Leeper, of
South Bend. The correspondence is as follows:

"St. Louis, October 21, 1846.

FRIEND COLFAX: It may not be wholly uninteresting to many of
your readers to know something of the progress of the Miami emigration
from the Wabash in Indiana to the country allotted to them by the government on the Osage, near the Missouri River under the direction and
immediate control of our townsman, Alexis Coquillard, truly "the great
Indian man" of the West. The history of the gathering and departure
of the Indians is about this: The time had expired in which they had
agreed to remove west under the treaty of 1840, and last spring they
were notified that a compliance with the stipulation of the treaty must
be had, and in a council in April they agreed in a few weeks to com-
mence the work of preparation. An examination of claims against the
Indians under the commissioners, selected partly by the Indians and
partly by the traders, took place, which detained the matter some six
weeks. On the sixth of June they met in council and agreed again, with
solemn assurances, that if they could be indulged until the first of
August, they would be all in readiness and start. This was granted
them by their paying half the expense accruing during that time; but
on the first of August they still remained *in statu quo*, and on the 19th
of that month firmly refused to emigrate. giving various reasons, one
of which was that the government should agree to pay the claims allowed
by the commissioners in money. This the government had refused already with as little ceremony as Gen. Taylor used in giving Ampudia
until one o'clock to comply with his demand of surrender at Monterey.

This, as had been well enough known before by many, showed the poor Indians were the dupes of a set of corrupt traders who made the Indians believe it would be dishonest to go off without arranging about their debts, and that the president would not use force to compel the execution and fulfillment of the treaty of 1840. The presence of a company of U. S. soldiers, however, very soon realized to the poor Indians (who are chargeable with all the extra expense), the falsity of the assurances of those *interested* friends, and the truth of their *real* ones. They immediately consented to go, and in ten days were on their way. They left Peru, Indiana, on the 6th inst. in canal boats by way of the Wabash and Erie and Miami canals; arrived at Cincinnati, where they took steamboat and reached here yesterday. Tomorrow they will start up the Missouri on the steamer Clermont. The boat from Cincinnati was much delayed by extreme low water. The captain of the Clermont allows more than double the usual time to make the trip up the Missouri for the same reason. The city papers make beautiful work in their reports of the arrival of the emigrating party. One of them gives an interesting history of the Miami Indians now here under the direction of "Mr. Cutran." It will no doubt pass through a number of journals as "an interesting sketch," and its verity scarcely doubted, although fabulous. It would be amusing to see the various manners in which Mr. Coquillard's name is written by persons ignorant of the true way. They are as numerous and droll as they used to get up on Chicago, and which were amusingly going the rounds of the papers. It is "Cutran," "Cuttan," "Cartran," etc., etc., never imagining it to be Coquillard.

There were ten Indians died on the passage. The Indian agent, Major Sinclair, of Ft. Wayne, as superintending agent on the part of the government, and Major Edson, also of Ft. Wayne, one of the contractors, also accompanied the emigration. Major Sinclair is known as formerly a member of the State legislature.   Yours truly,   J."

On November 9, 1846, the same correspondent wrote as follows from the "Indian Country:"

"A trip up the Missouri River at low stage of water is certainly one of the greatest bores that can be perpetrated upon a poor mortal, but when to its usual horrors is added the comfort of being cooped up with 350 filthy Indians and the usual number of hangers-on, within the limits of a small boat, with straw beds, straw pillows, your head against one partition and your feet against another, and all other accommodations in strict accordance therewith, traveling twenty-five to forty-five miles a day and tying up at night, you may presume that comfort finds no place there.

We arrived at Westport Landing with the Miami emigrating Indians on the morning of the first of November, 420 miles by river from St.

Louis, and to the country alloted to them, on the fifth. There were four
deaths of Indian children after we left St. Louis, and the wonder is that
there were not many more. The disposition and habits of the Indians
wholly unfit them for water emigration, and I am fully satisfied that
under no circumstances can an Indian be so comfortable in the white
man's boat as upon his mother earth, and in his native forest or prairie.

The country from Kansas (called Westport Landing at the mouth of
the Kansas river) to this place, about fifty-five miles directly south, is as
handsome, and, I doubt not, as fertile as can be found anywhere. It is
nearly all a rich, rolling, well-watered prairie. There is sufficient timber, in connection with coal, for fences and fuel. The Miamis are at
their new homes, well fixed, well satisfied, and but for the two great
curses—traders and whiskey—they might be a happy people. Their
land is excellent—plenty of prairie timber, water and stone; good game,
fish and wild fruit.   Yours,   J."

What W. W. Hill Remembers of the Miami Removal.

WILLIAM W. HILL, now and for many years past a citizen of Plymouth, was, at the time of the removal above noted, a resident of Miami
county and was present at the time the Indians were being congregated,
and was there the day they started. He says there was some dissatisfaction among the Indians in regard to the adjustment of their accounts,
and they determined not to go until a satisfactory settlement was made.
Thereupon the government sent a company of soldiers from Newport
barracks, near Cincinnati, whose presence soon satisfied the Indians
that the only course left was for them to arrange to go peaceably. The
soldiers remained until the Indians were started on their long journey,
when they returned to the barracks at Newport. The Indians, Mr.
Hill says, were loaded on canal boats and taken east on the Wabash and
Erie canal to the intersection of the canal running south through Celina,
Ohio, thence to Cincinnati, and there shipped by boat down the Ohio river.

Mr. Hill was well acquainted with many of the tribe, and in the
early times talked fluently the language of the Miamis. He was especially well acquainted with Gabriel Godfroy, the last lineal descendent
of the Miamis, still living near Peru. They are about the same age,
and were playfellows together for many years during their boyhood
days. Godfroy and his band, he says, retained their reservation, settled
down to peaceful persuits, and have got on in the world as well as their
white bretaren.

Gabriel Godfroy, the Miami Chief.

GABRIEL GODFROY, since the recent death of Pokagon, is the most distinguished Indian in the northwest. According to a recent correspond-

ent, although more than three score of years of age, he is still a fine specimen of manhood. He is short and stout, has a piercing black eye, a quick step and is well educated. A heavy growth of snow-white hair covers his head and hangs to his shoulders, and together with his swarthy countenance it produces a very picturesque appearance.

Chief Godfroy, as he is more familiarly known about home, owns one of the finest farms in northern Indiana, and as he looks after it himself it is cared for in the most successful manner. Surrounding him at home is his wife and several small children, the youngest not more than a year old. In the neighborhood are hundreds of Miami Indians, who very frequently look to Chief Godfroy for all kinds of advice and assistance. It is said without any exception he is guardian for more persons than any individual in the north central states.

Chief Godfroy has tried to trace his ancestors, but he failed to ascertain much concerning them. However, he has learned that his grandfather was a white man and was captured by the Suwanee Indians near Louisville, Ky., when he was but seven years of age. The boy grew up among the red-skins and became one of the most skillful traders of the tribe. He was the interpreter at the treaty of Greenville. He chose for a wife a woman who was half French but she belonged to the Miami tribe. To them were born many children, and at a ripe old age the father died near the place where he was captured when a boy. The mother and her children moved to Ft. Wayne to live among her people, and while there one of her daughters married Francis Godfroy, a Miami chief, whose father was a full-blooded Frenchman. Only a few children resulted from this union, and one of them was Gabriel Godfroy, the subject of this sketch.

THE RIVER STYX.

After the removal of the Indians, Jerry Smith was sent out by the government to survey the lands in Northern Indiana secured by the various treaties from the Pottawattomie Indians. The Menominee, Aubenaube, Naswaugee and other reserves in Marshall county, and the Kankakee reservations in LaPorte, Starke, Pulaski, Porter and Lake counties on the west, were all surveyed and properly laid off into sections and smaller divisions by him. He was an educated man, well read in ancient literature and the classics, and, besides, had a large vein of humor running through his mental organization. Those who were familiar with the Kankakee swamps in the region of the mouth of Yellow River will appreciate the following introduction by Jerry Smith to the report of his survey of this part of the lands ceded to the government by the Pottawattomie Indians. He says:

"That the River Styx is a fabled stream and that it never existed except in the brain of ancient poets and priests is a proposition which I am now fully prepared to deny and disprove; that Charon ever existed, ever kept a boat and ferry landing; that the dreary region of which ancient poets speak and through which the souls of the unburied wandered for one hundred years before his majesty of the frail bark would give them passage, and that the Elysian fields, where the souls of the just reveled in never-ending scenes of pleasure and delight, are imaginary regions, are equally false.

"The Kankakee, as it slops over Indiana and eastern Illinois, is the ancient Archeron, and English lake is the Stygian pool, at the head of which, near the line between ranges 3 and 4, still remain indisputable evidence of Charon's existence, of the identical spot where he so often landed his boat and took on board the souls of the departed, and last, but most of all, as a precious relic of antiquity which would make even an ordinary antiquarian leap with ecstasy of joy, the very paddle of the old gentleman is in existence.

"The dreary regions from the mouth of Markum's creek to the head of English lake, and particularly about the mouth of Yellow river, is where so many poor souls have wandered their one hundred years – and, in fact, as the use of the magnetic needle was not then known, I am not surprised at it taking a poor man so long to get out of that place when he was once fairly set into it without compass, chart, grog or tobacco. The 'Door Prairie' and the smaller ones about it, I take it to be what remains of the Elysian fields. What has become of its ancient occupants and why the order of things has changed, both in the Elysian fields and the Stygian pool, neither the present natives along the Kankakee, nor the owners, pre-emptioners and occupants of 'Door prairie' could tell me. I leave this to be ferreted out by historical societies and future antiquarians, having myself done sufficient to render me immortal by finding the prototype of the long-lost Styx, Charon's ferry landing, etc., without telling what has become of the old gentleman.

"To have a correct idea of the township the ancient poets should be well studied. Everything said by them respecting the nether regions and the abode of the wicked should be applied to it, and the whole will make a correct, faithful and true description thereof. The very thought of it makes my blood run cold."

THE POTTAWATTOMIE INDIANS IN COURSE OF ULTIMATE EXTINCTION.

By an act approved July 21, 1852, Congress appropriated $22,500 for the expenses and removal of the Pottawattomies of Indiana, and agent J. W. Whitefield reported on October 3, 1853, as follows:

" Much complaint is made by the Pottawattomies in getting their their accounts settled with the government. Quite a number say they furnished their own transportation and subsistence when they emigrated to their present homes, under a promise from the government officers that they would be paid. Others complain that their reservations in Indiana, Illinois and Michigan have been taken without compensation. I would respectfully suggest that their claims for emigrating should be sent to the states from which they removed to find out the true condition of their lands."

In the annual report of 1855, G. W. Clark reported as follows:

" According to the roll of 1854, there were 3,440 Pottawattomies on the reserve. There are about 250 others living among the Kickapoos, some of whom have intermarried in that tribe, and all of whom obstinately refuse to move to the Pottawattomie reserve. There are a few scattering families in Indiana, Illinois and Michigan, and among Sacs and Foxes. From all I can learn, this once numerous tribe cannot number, in all quarters, over 4,000 souls. The Pottawattomies complain greatly at the neglect of the government to reimburse those who furnished their own transportation and subsistance when they emigrated to this country. There are several hundred that set up claims of this character."

The late Simon Pokagon, who died January 27, 1899, since the publication of the foregoing sketches, in a late magazine article on the future of the Pottawattomies, said:

" As to the future of our race, it seems to me almost certain that in time it will lose its identity by amalgamation with the dominant race. No matter how distasteful it may seem to us, we are compelled to consider it as a probable result. Sensitive white people can console themselves, however, with the fact that there are today in the United States thousands of men and women of high social standing whose forefathers on one side were full blooded so-called savages, and yet the society in which they move, and in many cases they themselves, are ignorant of the fact. All white people are not ashamed of Indian blood; in fact, a few are proud of it.

"I do not wish it to be understood that I advocate or desire the amalgamation of our people with the white race. But I speak of it as an event that is almost certain, and we had much better rock with the boat that bears us on, than fight against the inevitable. I am frequently asked:

"'Pokagon, do you believe that the white man and the red man were originally of one blood?'

"My reply has been: I do not know, but from the present outlook they will be.

"The index finger of the past and present is pointing to the future, showing most conclusively that by the middle of the next century, all Indian reservations will have passed away. Then our people will begin to scatter, and the result will be a general mixing of the races. By intermarriage, the blood of our people, like the waters that flow into the great ocean, will be forever lost in that of the dominant race, and generations yet unborn will read in history of the red men of the forest, and inquire, 'Where are they?'"

THE GOVERNMENT'S INDIAN POLICY.

In his annual message to congress on December 3, 1838, President Van Buren, upon congratulating the country on the successful removal of the Indians to the Western reservation, took occasion to set forth explicitly the policy long established in regard to Indian affairs, for the purpose of exonerating the government of the United States from the undeserved reproach which had been cast upon it through several successive administrations. His elucidation of the subject, succinctly and fairly stating the uniform policy of the government, is deemed a fitting conclusion to this narrative. This policy never contemplated the use of force in the removal of the Indians, and it is to be regretted that the Governor of Indiana deemed it necessary to use soldiers in removing the Pottawattomies from Marshall county, the only case of the kind, so far as is known, in the entire history of our perplexing Indian affairs. President Van Buren said:

"That a mixed occupancy of the same territory by the white and red man is incompatible with the safety or happiness of either, is a position in respect to which there has long since ceased to be room for difference of opinion. Reason and experience have alike demonstrated its impracticability. The bitter fruits of every attempt heretofore to overcome the barriers interposed by nature have only been destructive, both physically and morally, to the Indian; dangerous conflicts of authority between the federal and state governments, and detrimental to the individual prosperity of the citizen, as well as to the general improvement of the country. The remedial policy, the principles of which were settled more than thirty years ago under the administration of Mr. Jefferson, consists of an extinction, for a fair consideration, of the titles to all the lands still occupied by the Indians within the states and territories of the United States, their removal to a country west of the Mississippi much more extensive and better adapted to their condition than that in which they then resided; the guarantee to them by the United States of their exclusive possession of that country forever, exempt from all intrusions by white men, with ample provision against external violence and internal dissentions, and the extension to them of suitable facilities for their advancement in civilization. This has not been the policy of particular administrations only, but of each in succession, since the first attempt to carry it out under that of Mr. Monroe. All have labored for its accomplishment, only with different success.

The manner of its execution has, it is true, from time to time given rise to conflicts of opinion and unjust imputation; but in respect to the wisdom and necessity of the policy itself, there has not from the beginning existed a doubt in the mind of any calm, judicious, disinterested friend of the Indian race accustomed to reflection and enlightened by experience.

"Occupying the double character of contractor on its own account, and guardian for the parties contracted with, it was hardly to be expected that the dealings of the federal government with the Indians would escape misrepresentation. That there occurred in the early settlement of this country, as in all others where the civilized race has succeeded to the possessions of the savage, instances of oppression and fraud on the part of the former there is too much reason to believe. No such offenses can, however, be justly charged upon this government since it became free to pursue its own course. Its dealings with the Indian tribes have been just and friendly throughout: its efforts for their civilization constant, and directed by the best feelings of humanity: its watchfulness in protecting them from individual frauds unremitting; its forbearance under the keenest provocations, the deepest injuries, and the most flagrant outrages, may challenge at least a comparison with any nation, ancient or modern, in similar circumstances; and if in future times a powerful, civilized and happy nation of Indians shall be found to exist within the limits of the Northern continent, it will be owing to the consummation of that policy which has been so unjustly assailed. Certain it is that the transactions of the federal government with the Indians have been uniformly characterized by a sincere and paramount desire to promote their welfare; and it must be a source of the highest gratification to every friend to justice and humanity to learn that, notwithstanding the obstructions from time to time thrown in its way, and the difficulties which have arisen from the peculiar and impracticable nature of the Indian character, the wise, humane and undeviating policy of the government in this, the most difficult of all our relations, foreign or domestic, has at length been justified to the world in its near approach to a happy and certain consummation."

www.ingramcontent.com/pod-product-compliance
Lightning Source LLC
Chambersburg PA
CBHW020337090426
42735CB00009B/1568